MOTIVATIONAL INTERVIEWING
IN SOCIAL WORK PRACTICE

APPLICATIONS OF MOTIVATIONAL INTERVIEWING

Stephen Rollnick, William R. Miller, and Theresa B. Moyers,
Series Editors

Since the publication of Miller and Rollnick's classic *Motivational Interviewing*, now in its third edition, MI has been widely adopted as a tool for facilitating change. This highly practical series includes general MI resources as well as books on specific clinical contexts, problems, and populations. Each volume presents powerful MI strategies that are grounded in research and illustrated with concrete, "how-to-do-it" examples.

Motivational Interviewing in Health Care:
Helping Patients Change Behavior
Stephen Rollnick, William R. Miller, and Christopher C. Butler

Building Motivational Interviewing Skills: A Practitioner Workbook
David B. Rosengren

Motivational Interviewing with Adolescents and Young Adults
Sylvie Naar-King and Mariann Suarez

Motivational Interviewing in Social Work Practice
Melinda Hohman

Motivational Interviewing in the Treatment of Anxiety
Henny A. Westra

Motivational Interviewing, Third Edition: Helping People Change
William R. Miller and Stephen Rollnick

Motivational Interviewing in Groups
Christopher C. Wagner and Karen S. Ingersoll, with Contributors

Motivational Interviewing in the Treatment
of Psychological Problems, Second Edition
Hal Arkowitz, William R. Miller, and Stephen Rollnick, Editors

Motivational Interviewing in Diabetes Care
Marc P. Steinberg and William R. Miller

Motivational Interviewing in Nutrition and Fitness
Dawn Clifford and Laura Curtis

MOTIVATIONAL INTERVIEWING IN SOCIAL WORK PRACTICE

Melinda Hohman

Series Editors' Note by
William R. Miller and Stephen Rollnick

THE GUILFORD PRESS
New York   London

© 2012 The Guilford Press
A Division of Guilford Publications, Inc.
370 Seventh Avenue, Suite 1200, New York, NY 10001
www.guilford.com

Paperback edition 2016

Printed in the United States of America

This book is printed on acid-free paper.

Last digit is print number: 9 8 7 6 5 4 3

The author has checked with sources believed to be reliable in her efforts to provide
information that is complete and generally in accord with the standards of practice that
are accepted at the time of publication. However, in view of the possibility of human
error or changes in behavioral, mental health, or medical sciences, neither the author, nor
the editor and publisher, nor any other party who has been involved in the preparation
or publication of this work warrants that the information contained herein is in every
respect accurate or complete, and they are not responsible for any errors or omissions or
the results obtained from the use of such information. Readers are encouraged to confirm
the information contained in this book with other sources.

Library of Congress Cataloging-in-Publication Data

Hohman, Melinda.
  Motivational interviewing in social work practice / Melinda Hohman.
    p. cm. — (Applications of motivational interviewing)
  Includes bibliographical references and index.
  ISBN 978-1-60918-969-3 (hardcover)
  ISBN 978-1-4625-2369-6 (paperback)
  1. Social service.   2. Interviewing in social service.   3. Motivational
interviewing.   I. Title.
  HV40.H629 2012
  361.3′22—dc23
                                                        2011019750

For Jerry, Lauren, and Eric—my motivators

About the Author

Melinda Hohman, PhD, MSW, is Professor in the School of Social Work at San Diego State University, where she has taught since 1995. She teaches courses in social work practice, substance abuse treatment, and motivational interviewing, both at the graduate and undergraduate level. Dr. Hohman's research interests include substance abuse assessment and treatment services and the overlap of substance abuse treatment and child welfare services. She has been a trainer in motivational interviewing since 1999, training community social workers, child welfare workers, probation officers, and addiction counselors across the United States.

Contributing Authors

Elizabeth Barnett, MSW, is a doctoral student in the Department of Preventive Medicine at the University of Southern California. She is an active member of the Motivational Interviewing Network of Trainers and a researcher of motivational interviewing. Her interests include adolescent substance use and juvenile justice.

Mike Eichler, MSW, is a faculty member in the School of Social Work at San Diego State University. He also directs the Consensus Organizing Center, which trains students to help low-income communities by building relationships based on mutual self-interest.

Rhoda Emlyn-Jones, MA, DipSW.CQSW, OBE, is service manager for Social Services in South Wales, United Kingdom. She has developed and managed a range of social services for people who experience homelessness and for people who have drug- and alcohol-related difficulties, and has developed innovative services designed to address all families' needs in a single intervention. In 2007 Ms. Emlyn-Jones was named Welsh Woman of the Year for services to the disadvantaged and vulnerable.

Bill James, LCSW, is a protective services supervisor for the County of San Diego and has worked in child welfare since 1993. His focus has been on foster youth with mental health challenges and their families. He started working to integrate motivational interviewing into child welfare practice in 2006.

Hilda Loughran, PhD, is Lecturer in the College of Human Sciences School of Applied Social Science at University College Dublin. Her areas of interest include social work education, counseling and research, and alcohol and drug policy. Dr. Loughran's most recent research projects include work in the areas of alcohol use, crisis pregnancy, community drug issues, and brief interventions.

Sally Mathiesen, PhD, LCSW, is Associate Professor of Social Work and a Fulbright Scholar at San Diego State University. Her research agenda is focused on mental health over the lifespan, including co-occurring disorders (COD). Her recent research includes exploring acceptability of an evidence-based model for COD in international settings and evidence-based practice in international social work education.

Audrey M. Shillington, PhD, MSW, is Professor of Social Work and Associate Director of the Center for Alcohol and Drug Studies at San Diego State University. She has written over 50 peer-reviewed publications and has been a principal investigator or co-investigator on funded research focusing on alcohol and drug prevention with adolescents and young adults.

Katie Slack, MSW, is a member of the Motivational Interviewing Network of Trainers. She specializes in the use of motivational interviewing with domestic violence, child welfare, and health coaching. Ms. Slack is the owner of MI Training Today, a motivational interviewing training company with training locations in San Diego, California, and Nashville, Tennessee.

Cristine Urquhart, MSW, RSW, is a member of the international Motivational Interviewing Network of Trainers and founder of Change Talk Associates. She works with governmental organizations and health services across Canada to integrate motivational interviewing into current practice and improve health outcomes.

Stéphanie Wahab, PhD, MSW, is Associate Professor in the School of Social Work at Portland State University. Her teaching and research interests are informed by anti-oppressive practice and include gender-based violence, commercial sex work, motivational interviewing, and participatory and qualitative methods of inquiry.

Series Editors' Note

Social work and motivational interviewing (MI) seem to be a natural fit. At the heart of social work is a desire to empower people, to see and call upon their own strengths and abilities. Social workers accomplish this primarily through talking, and a skillful sensitivity to language is central within MI. Key elements of the underlying spirit of MI also converge with core values of social work: a compassionate empathy for those we serve, a practical and collaborative partnership, and a hopeful intention to call forth the best in others.

MI began as a way to help people find their way out of alcohol problems, but it soon became apparent that this counseling style has much wider applicability. MI is particularly useful in situations where people want or need to make a change but are ambivalent about doing so. The change might be in behavior, attitude, or lifestyle. Part of them knows that change is important, and another part is reluctant. They want it but they don't want it simultaneously. That is a very normal human dilemma. Ambivalence is, in fact, one step forward on the road to change.

MI is not about fixing people. It does not come from a deficit view that people are lacking something that we need to install. Ultimately, people are free to choose what they will do and how they will be. MI is about helping people find their own personal motivation for positive change, which leads naturally to planning and connecting them with the resources they need to accomplish it. That facilitator role is a natural one for social workers.

We are delighted, then, with the publication of this very first volume on MI within the profession of social work. We hope that it will stimulate further creativity and research in the applications of MI to the broad range of services that social workers provide.

WILLIAM R. MILLER, PhD
STEPHEN ROLLNICK, PhD

Preface

Thirteen-plus years ago I read *Motivational Interviewing: Preparing People to Change Addictive Behavior* (Miller & Rollnick, 1991) and fell in love with motivational interviewing (MI), a communication method to assist people who are struggling with change. While very hard to learn and practice, MI made intuitive sense to me as a respectful, client-centered approach to clients and as a research-based intervention to help them think through their concerns and ways of addressing them. I immediately added content on MI to my social work practice and addiction treatment courses. My students embraced it enthusiastically as well and wanted more information.

This book is based on my subsequent years of teaching and training MI, particularly with social work students and social workers in the community. I wanted to provide information about and examples of the skills and spirit of MI that are useful to social workers in their everyday work lives. The case examples are set across the micro, mezzo, and macro settings of social work practice in order to meet the needs of various readers as well as to indicate how MI can be integrated into different contexts of social work interventions. While this book may be useful to other professionals as well, my goal was to utilize the lens of social work concepts and values that guide the profession. I called on the resources and knowledge of social workers, both across the United States and internationally, to assist writing many of the chapters, drawing on their expertise in MI but also in mental health, intimate partner violence, school social work, and community organizing.

I have expanded on some of the concepts proposed by Miller and Rollnick (1991, 2002) that enhance the learning process and I have also kept the core principles and methods for practicing MI. I hope that readers will find this book a useful tool in learning this humanistic method of communicating with clients.

ACKNOWLEDGMENTS

I want to thank all of my contributors, who lent their expertise, time, and hard work. Thank you, too, to William R. Miller and Stephen Rollnick for their suggestions, ideas, and editing. I appreciate those who assisted me in the process of writing this book: Ray DiCiccio, John Kleinpeter, Amalia Hernandez, Jodi Palamides, and Ali Hall, coder extraordinaire, who reviewed all of the coding of the dialogues. I am grateful to all the members of the Motivational Interviewing Network of Trainers, who readily share their ideas and expertise. Finally, I want to thank my family for all of their encouragement and support.

Contents

1

Why Social Work
and Motivational Interviewing?

Social workers love to talk. And it is a good thing that we love to do it. Other than the dreaded paperwork, it is what we do all day long: interview clients, consult with colleagues, meet with families, present cases at team meetings, go to lunch with a friend, and perhaps teach a class of social work students. We take phone calls from worried parents, mediate problems between middle school students, present information in court, run support groups or therapy groups, advocate with legislators, find beds for homeless clients, and recruit volunteers to be mentors. Though social workers work in many different kinds of settings, we have in common that we spend most of our time talking.

We think we are pretty good at talking; why, we have been doing it for years! No one has to teach us how to communicate. Sure, we learned a bit about interviewing skills in social work school and, as students, we watched our field instructors interact with clients. But for the most part, as in parenting, we tend to rely on communication skills that we developed in growing up and have used all along.

Sometimes, though, as social workers, we run into clients that we find particularly challenging, and it seems the usual methods of communication aren't that helpful. Clients may be angry, argumentative, or apathetic, seem-

1

ing to have no desire to change despite being on an obvious (to us) destructive course. When this happens, it is easy for any of us to try to persuade or even argue with clients. Sometimes we feel responsible for our clients and the outcome and react by trying to fix the problem. It feels like if we could only give them enough information, ask the right questions, or lay out the consequences of a particular action, then clients would be open to change or at least, to calm down. This can especially occur in situations that have a dire outcome, such as in child welfare or probation. Research has borne this out as well: a study of interviewing skills of child welfare social workers in the United Kingdom found low levels of listening and empathy and high levels of confrontation. The social workers tended to set the agenda for client interviews without ever asking what the clients wanted to discuss (Forrester, McCambridge, Waissbein, & Rollnick, 2008). No doubt they felt extremely responsible for making sure that their clients made the right choices and resorted to providing direction for change.

Often the context or the culture of our practice setting influences how we communicate. My first job was working in juvenile probation, and my role models there taught me how to be direct and blunt. From there I worked in adolescent drug treatment, where the model was to be very directive and challenging until clients accepted the label of "alcoholic" or "drug addict." This confrontation was seen as necessary for clients to break through their "denial" and admit to a problem. Counselors or social workers in both of these settings were viewed as experts who had the answers and had to warn, admonish, threaten, or advise. This was taking the "usual" or directive communication method to an extreme.

Although I was able to do this fairly well, a part of me was always a bit uncomfortable with it, as it seemed so removed from what I was taught in my Bachelor of Social Work and Master of Social Work programs regarding the values of the social work profession: service, respect for the client, nonjudgmental, determination, dignity and worth of the person, and the importance of human relationships. Besides advocating for social justice and working across systems, social workers are called to work as partners with their clients, to recognize and emphasize their clients' strengths, and to assist clients in meeting their own needs (International Federation of Social Work [IFSW], 2004; Wahab, 2005a). Social workers by nature seem to be drawn to humanistic approaches.

It was entirely by happenstance that I discovered motivational interviewing (MI). I became a social work educator in 1995, and a few years later was looking for additional resources for the substance abuse course I was teaching to graduate students. I came across *Motivational Interviewing:*

Preparing People to Change Addictive Behavior (Miller & Rollnick, 1991) and found that the concepts and methods described in this book for working with those with substance use problems were much more congruent with social work values as well as with my own personal value system. Bill Miller, one of the authors of this book, once told me, "Clinicians seem to recognize it when they see it." Not only was MI intuitively appealing, but at that time strong research to support it was beginning to accumulate. I immediately began to integrate MI into my class, and students responded well to it. I began to think of other areas of practice where MI might be useful, and applied it to child welfare work for substance using parents, as I was quite interested in this area (Hohman, 1998). I was trained as an MI trainer in 1999 and integrated MI concepts and skills into social work practice skills courses. With strong support of MI as an evidence-based practice, like other schools of social work across the country, my department now offers both undergraduate and graduate courses that are strictly about MI.

WHAT IS MI?

MI has been defined as "a client-centered, directive method for enhancing intrinsic motivation to change by exploring and resolving ambivalence" (Miller & Rollnick, 2002, p. 25). It has been framed as a "guiding" style of communication as compared to a more "directive" style (Miller & Rollnick, 2009). Initially developed as an alternative to the confrontational and advice-giving methods of alcohol use disorder treatment, it has been expanded and applied to a variety of health-related behaviors and other concerns. Social workers have applied MI in areas such as:

- Work with adolescents in school settings (Kaplan, Engle, Austin, & Wagner, 2011; Smith, Hall, Jang, & Arndt, 2009; Velasquez et al., 2009)
- Colorectal screening (Wahab, Menon, & Szalacha, 2008)
- Reduction of HIV/AIDS transmission (Picciano, Roffman, Kalichman, & Walke, 2007; Rutledge, 2007)
- Interpersonal violence (Dia, Simmons, Oliver, & Cooper, 2009; Motivational Interviewing & Intimate Partner Violence Workgroup, 2010; Wahab, 2006)
- Vocational rehabilitation (Manthey, 2009; Manthey, Jackson, & Evans-Brown, 2010)

- Homeless young women (Wenzel, D'Amico, Barnes, & Gilbert, 2009)
- Exercise for patients with multiple sclerosis (Smith et al., 2010)
- Older adults (Cummings, Cooper, & Cassie, 2009)
- Driving under the influence (DUI) clients (DiStefano & Hohman, 2007)
- Child welfare clients (Forrester, McCambridge, Waissbein, Emlyn-Jones, & Rollnick, 2007; Hohman & Salsbury, 2009; Jasiura, Hunt, & Urquhart, in press)
- Clients receiving alcohol and other drug treatment (Cloud et al., 2006)
- Criminal justice clients (Clark, 2006)
- Prevention of fetal alcohol spectrum disorders (Urquhart & Jasiura, 2010)

MI is a style or "way of being" with clients as well as a set of specific skills that are used to convey empathy and encourage clients to consider and plan change. Building on the work of Carl Rogers's client-centered therapy (Rogers, 1951), MI is founded on three aspects that constitute the "spirit" of MI: *collaboration*, *evocation*, and *autonomy support* (Miller & Rollnick, 2002). The collaboration aspect suggests that social workers are seen as partners working with clients to understand their goals, motivators, and ambivalence around certain behavior changes. Social workers are not experts but guides. We can provide information or advice, with clients' consent. It is assumed that clients have what they need to make changes.

Grant Corbett, a social worker, calls this the *competence worldview*, as compared to the *deficit worldview* (Corbett, 2009). In the deficit world-view, social workers view their clients as not having the resources, skills, or characteristics to make changes. They need to have these things given or instilled in them. They lack insight or knowledge and we, as "expert" social workers, need to give them information, advise them, or teach skills. Social workers can operate from the deficit worldview even when using the strengths perspective (Corbett, 2009; Saleeby, 2006) by unconsciously indicating to clients that if they work hard enough, they will find the hidden strengths that clients have. It is up to the social worker to discover them. In the competence worldview, clients are seen as already having the resources and characteristics they need, and it is our task to evoke from clients their thoughts, ideas, abilities, and ways to change.

The aspect of evocation supports our eliciting or drawing out from clients their thoughts and ideas regarding goals and methods of change.

Clients are not seen as being "in denial" but as wrestling with ambivalence regarding changing a certain behavior. For instance, a mother involved with the child welfare system may enjoy the energy or escape that using methamphetamine gives her, and she has a desire to be a good parent as well. Working in a guiding fashion, the social worker evokes from the client her own motivation for change in a specific area that may include what her thoughts might be on becoming a better parent, one of her values.

The third aspect undergirding MI is autonomy support. Clients are ultimately the ones who make their decisions. We cannot force them to do anything, even with warnings or threats. Thus, MI practitioners do not use coercive methods and understand that clients ultimately choose what they think is best for themselves, even if we don't agree with it. As given in the example above, a mother may choose drug use over her children. The social worker still has to support the best interests of the children, and perhaps even remove them from her care. Social workers may not always agree with choices clients make, but we have to keep in mind that clients are more prone to "push back" or prove their own autonomy when we engage with them using "usual" communication methods, like threats, warnings, and consequences (Catley et al., 2006; Hohman, Kleinpeter, & Loughran, 2005; Miller & Rose, 2009). We know these methods don't usually work; if they did, there would be no recidivism in our prisons. Or maybe, no need for prisons! Honoring clients' autonomy helps avoid resistance and encourage engagement in problem solving in a positive manner. When clients are on a destructive path, it is hard to resist the desire to fix the problem—by doing for them, or by warning or threatening. This desire (the "righting reflex") is discussed further in Chapter 5.

Are there any times when MI shouldn't be used? If a client has already decided to change, MI would not be needed, although client-centered skills in listening can be helpful. It is unethical for a practitioner who has a personal or professional vested interest in an outcome (such as trying to motivate a teen client to give a child up for adoption) to use specific motivational strategies (Miller & Rollnick, 2002). Could we use MI in crisis situations? While there is not much research in this area, some are indicating that it is possible (Loughran, 2011). Zerler (2009) and Britton, Williams, and Conner (2008) have proposed MI as a method to manage and intervene with suicidal clients through the development of a therapeutic alliance to engage in safety planning and discussion of the client's ambivalence about living. While this ambivalence can be painful to hear, Zerler asserts that using MI helps to build client autonomy and promotes self-efficacy to "make 'good choices' about 'bad feelings'" (p. 1208).

WHY USE MI IN SOCIAL WORK PRACTICE?

Social workers, and other helping professionals, are drawn to MI for a variety of reasons (Wahab, 2005b). The four main reasons appear to be that (1) the aspects and values in MI are similar to those that guide and are embraced by professional social workers; (2) MI has a rich body of evidence that supports its use with populations at risk and the other types of clients who typically interact with social workers; (3) MI has been found to be effective in clients from diverse backgrounds and settings and seems to fit well with concepts of cultural competency; and (4) MI has been found to blend well with other types of interventions.

Social Work Principles and MI Aspects

While there are social work codes of ethics in a variety of countries around the globe, most have the common themes of social workers being committed to social justice, serving diverse and marginalized populations, practicing with integrity, promoting client self-determination, maintaining confidentiality, and using science to guide practice (IFSW, 2004). Scheafor and Horejsi (2007) have synthesized much of this work into 24 common social work principles, with 17 of them being focused on those that guide practice work with clients.

MI is a method to use when what we hope for is behavior change. Table 1.1 lists those social work principles that would be most closely related to the type of work where MI would be used and to the related MI aspects/spirit. The social work principles include dignity, respect, individualization, vision, client strengths, client participation, self-determination, and empowerment. All of these principles would be consistent with the MI spirit of collaboration, evocation, and autonomy/support. Because MI is based on client-centered theory and approaches, clients are seen as the experts on their lives, with the role of the social worker being to collaborate on looking at thoughts and ways of addressing client-identified concerns. An MI interview looks deceptively simple as our clients do most of the talking; we are busy evoking the clients' perspective as well as keeping track of the responses for selected reflections and summaries. We may give advice with permission to do so, and typically advice is embedded in a menu of options that clients might choose from. Clients make their decisions regarding behavior change and how this will be accomplished, with their own determined methods. This helps build client empowerment and self-determination.

TABLE 1.1. The Relationship between Social Work Principles and MI Aspects

Social work principles (Scheafor & Horejsi, 2007)	MI aspects/spirit (Miller & Rollnick, 2002)
The social worker should treat the client with dignity.	MI spirit involves working *collaboratively* with clients as equal partners and avoiding labeling.
The social worker should individualize the client.	MI spirit involves *evoking* from the client their unique views and thoughts on their concerns.
The social worker should consider clients experts on their own lives.	MI is based on client-centered theory and approaches that value the knowledge that clients have about their own lives.
The social worker should lend vision to the client.	Supporting self-efficacy is a principle of MI whereby the social worker uses affirmations to emphasize strengths and highlights other changes clients have made on their own.
The social worker should build on client strengths.	In a competence worldview (Corbett, 2009), the task in MI is for the social worker to determine *what the client sees* as his or her strengths or abilities and how positive change has occurred in the past.
The social worker should maximize client participation.	In an MI interview, the client should be doing the majority of the talking, with the social worker *supporting client autonomy. Collaboration* means that change plans are created based on client needs and desires.
The social worker should maximize client self-determination.	Advice is given with client permission and is provided within a menu of options. Client capability and autonomy are emphasized regarding making choices.
The social worker should help the client learn self-directed problem-solving skills.	MI can be combined with other methods as needed, such as cognitive-behavioral therapy, *if* the client wants to learn problem-solving skills.
The social worker should maximize client empowerment.	The principle of supporting self-efficacy and autonomy support helps empower clients to ultimately be the ones to make decisions over their own lives.

MI as an Evidence-Based Practice and the Evidence-Based Process

As indicated earlier, codes of ethics have called on social workers to utilize science or research evidence in determining the best interventions for individual clients. The United States' accrediting body for schools of social work, the Council on Social Work Education (CSWE; 2001), requires that students learn how to use the best available evidence in their work. This is a change from the previous paradigm of authority-based practice, which valued tradition, experience, and advice from colleagues or supervisors (Mullen & Bacon, 2006; Proctor, 2006). Funders too are requiring social workers in agencies to utilize evidence-based practices. There are several resources for social workers to utilize, such as the California Evidence-Based Clearinghouse for Child Welfare (CEBC; 2006–2009), the National Registry of Evidence-Based Programs and Practices sponsored by the Substance Abuse and Mental Health Services Administration (NREPP; 2010), the Campbell Collaboration (C2; 2010), and the Cochrane Collaboration (2010). All have information about MI. The CEBC utilizes a scientific rating scale to determine how supported an intervention is by research. On this website, MI for parental substance abuse has the highest rating or a "1" or "well-supported by research evidence" (CEBC, 2006–2009). On the NREPP, MI received a 3.9 on a 4.0 scale regarding its effectiveness with alcohol and other drug use. This site also provides reviews of adaptations of MI. The Campbell and Cochrane sites provide systematic reviews of research of applications of MI to various topics, such as tobacco cessation.

Currently there are close to 300 studies of the use of MI to address various health and other behavioral changes (Moyers, Martin, Houck, Christopher, & Tonigan, 2009) (for a listing, see Rollnick, Miller, & Butler, 2008, or the MI website, *www.motivationalinterviewing.org*). Although MI has not been applied to every area of human concern, the broad application and depth of research in some areas are appealing to social workers who are looking to integrate evidence-based practice into their work. Models of how to do this through the evidence-based *process* stress the need to search for and critically appraise research and other information about specific interventions, perhaps by using the websites listed above, and to include the client in the decision making regarding which interventions to use (Gambrill, 2006). This could be done in an MI-congruent manner; however, MI should not be used to influence a client to move in a particular direction regarding the selection of an intervention.

MI as a Cross-Cultural Practice

Since the publication of the first edition of a book describing MI (Miller & Rollnick, 1991) and continuing evidence of research support across cultures, MI has been adopted by social workers and other helping professionals from around the world. William Miller and Stephen Rollnick's (2002) book, in its second edition, has been translated into 18 languages, and there are over 40 languages represented among MI trainers. The use of MI as an intervention has been studied with a variety of clients in the United States—for instance, with African Americans regarding diet and hypertension (Befort et al., 2008; Ogedegbe et al., 2007; Resnicow et al., 2001, 2008); Native Americans regarding alcohol use and HIV testing (Foley et al., 2005; Villanueva, Tonigan, & Miller, 2007); Latinos who received interventions for smoking cessation (Borrelli, McQuaid, Novak, Hammond, & Becker, 2010) and to increase psychotropic medication adherence (Anez, Silva, Paris, & Bedregal, 2008; Interian, Martinez, Rios, Krejci, & Guarnaccia, 2010); and Asian Americans to increase substance use treatment engagement (Yu, Clark, Chandra, Dias, & Lai, 2009). One meta-analysis of 72 research studies gave empirical support for MI as being effective cross culturally: treatment effects were almost double for minority clients across the studies than for nonminority clients (Hettema, Steele, & Miller, 2005).

The appeal of MI as a communication method that can be used in various cultures may be due to its focus on the recognition and utilization of the values, goals, and strategies of the client (Interian et al., 2010; Venner, Feldstein, & Tafoya, 2007) and its respect for the client's autonomy (Hettema, Steeler, & Miller, 2005). In MI, we suspend our own thoughts, goals, and values, and focus on intensely listening to and reflecting those of our clients. McRoy (2007) proposes that this is important in order to move beyond perspectives or even cultural stereotypes that we might hold. Motivations and strategies for change are evoked from the client and are not imposed by us (Miller, Villanueva, Tonigan, & Cuzmar, 2007). Minority clients may experience those of us who are from the majority culture as paternalistic when we impose goals and strategies based on our worldview. No matter what our race or ethnicity, in MI we strive to work against being the "experts" who provide knowledge and skills, for this only continues to perpetuate racism and power differentials, particularly with clients from oppressed groups (Sakamoto & Pitner, 2005). The spirit of MI, with its emphasis on collaboration, evocation, and autonomy support, may be one way to address racial, cultural, or class differences.

In order to be effective cross culturally, Sue (1998) proposes that social workers, therapists, or counselors should (1) be scientifically minded in that we test hypotheses about what we are hearing from clients on an individual basis and not make assumptions that all clients from a certain group are the same; (2) practice "dynamic sizing" in knowing when to apply knowledge about culture without stereotyping and when to frame what we are seeing or hearing as individuals to clients; and (3) have culturally specific knowledge about the population/culture where our clients are from, whether it is racial/ethnic, geographical, physical, or sexual orientation. Because we use MI to draw out and understand the clients' perspectives on a problem, their values and goals, and methods to achieve change, we learn about our clients' culture and their connection to that culture. Hypothesis testing can occur through the use of reflective listening and summaries to clients about what is important to them. If we are wrong in our hypothesis, most likely our clients will correct us and move on. An MI interview can be helpful in learning about a specific culture, but we should not expect our clients to "teach" us or be a spokesperson for a culture. We need to find other ways to learn about our clients'cultures (Sue, 1998). However, there is so much variability within racial/ethnic/cultural groups that MI helps us to recognize what is important to a particular client, and it may be different from our understanding of what to expect from members of that culture. Thus we use MI to individualize care for clients in the context of their view of and relationship to their culture.

How does MI get culturally adapted for larger groups of clients? As funders and agencies are moving toward the integration of evidence-based practices in client interventions, there is a need to take methods that have been shown to be effective in tightly controlled clinical trials and apply them to the real-life work of social workers in the community. It is also important to remain true to the method and still adapt it for specific racial or ethnic groups, in order to best meet their needs (Castro, Barrera, & Martinez, 2004). Making MI interventions appropriate for a particular culture can involve the use of focus groups made up of clients or representatives from the culture. Discussions of values and norms within a particular community as well as the use of language can help shape an intervention while keeping it true to its original design (Anez et al., 2008; Interian et al., 2010; Longshore & Grills, 2000; Venner, Feldstein, & Tafoya, 2007). For instance, an adaptation of MI for use with Native Americans (Venner, Feldstein, & Tafoya, 2006) emphasized respect, no use of labeling, and collaboration, all of which are congruent with Native American values and practices. Focus group participants indicated that helping clients find their own motivations and methods of change are extremely empowering (Venner et al., 2007).

MI Combines Well with Other Methods

Although MI can be used as a stand-alone intervention, it is also effective when it is combined with other intervention methods (Burke, Arkowitz,

& Menchola, 2003; Lundahl & Burke, 2009). It has been used as a pre-treatment intervention or used in combination with other methods, such as cognitive-behavioral therapy (CBT). MI has been modified or adapted for various settings. These adaptations include methods for conducting brief screening for alcohol problems. MI can be used as one method to achieve goals within a larger intervention—for instance, to engage parents in parent skills training or family group conferencing meetings.

Studies have found that an MI interview conducted before clients enter treatment (such as for substance use, for co-occurring disorders, or for intimate violence perpetrators) will increase program attendance and engagement (Carroll, Libby, Sheehan, & Hyland, 2001; Carroll et al., 2006; Daley, Salloum, Zuckoff, Kirisci, & Thase, 1998; Musser & Murphy, 2009; Musser, Semiatin, Taft, & Murphy, 2008). However, a recent meta-analysis found only a slight advantage to using MI when compared to treatment as usual in treatment engagement (Lundahl, Kunz, Tollefson, Brownell, & Burke, 2010). In these pretreatment MI interviews, clients are asked to discuss what their concerns are and what they would like to get from treatment. Providing the opportunity for clients to "tell their story" and to set treatment goals allows clients to engage with the social worker/agency due to the personalized focus and autonomy support. Typically when these pretreatment interviews are studied, clients are compared to "treatment as usual" clients who enter treatment without such an interview but have a standard intake/evaluation interview. Standard interviews include gathering of information from clients such as their substance use history and current concerns, often done with a battery of paperwork and forms. This is a subset of the "usual" communication methods, whereby the state/agency/social worker deems what is important to know and the interviewer asks a lot questions to get that information. MI interviews have also been inserted during the treatment process as clients are ready to move from one level of care to another (Zweben & Zuckoff, 2002). For instance, MI can be used to increase attendance at Alcoholics Anonymous with substance use clients who are leaving treatment and are ambivalent about participating in this or other 12-step programs (Cloud et al., 2006).

MI has been combined with other intervention methods, most often CBT. Corcoran (2005), a social worker, proposed the strengths and skills model whereby MI was combined with CBT and solution-focused therapy (SFT) for a variety of client problems. In this model, the social worker uses MI and SFT to engage clients and learn of their concerns and motivators; as ambivalence is reduced, the social worker switches over to the discussion of the clients' strategies for change with role plays, which is consistent with

CBT work. MI combined with CBT for alcohol dependence (and along with medication) was studied in the large-scale Project COMBINE multi-site clinical trial (Longabaugh, Zweben, Locastro, & Miller, 2005). This model used MI to engage the client and then focused on areas for relapse prevention that included skill development and rehearsal, all while maintaining the spirit of MI (Miller, 2004).

Motivational enhancement therapy (MET) is a version of MI whereby clients receive some sort of normative feedback about the behavior under discussion, such as alcohol or drug use, condom use, and smoking, along with MI (Burke, Arkowitz, & Menchola, 2003). Screening and brief interventions (SBI) are interviews that take place usually in primary care or an emergency department of a hospital and that use MI within a structured format. With permission, patients are screened, usually about alcohol use, are provided feedback about the severity of their score compared with national norms, and are asked to consider ways to cut back alcohol use in a supportive and collaborative manner. This takes about 15 to 30 minutes and studies of this intervention have consistently demonstrated reductions in alcohol misuse at 6-month follow-up (Bernstein et al., 2007; Madras et al., 2009). Other brief interventions can take place over a few sessions, such as the work done by John Baer and colleagues with homeless youth in Seattle. Using MI, youth were screened regarding substance use and provided with feedback on topics of their own choosing such as substance use norms, symptoms of substance dependence, motivation to change, and/or personal goals. This was done over four short sessions in an attempt to reduce client drug use and increase utilization of social services. Those who received the intervention, as compared to a control group, increased their use of services, but substance use declined for both groups over time (Baer, Garrett, Beadnell, Wells, & Peterson, 2007). See Chapter 7 for more information on MI with adolescents.

MI is also used to obtain a goal within a different intervention, such as parent skills training. Parent skills training typically uses CBT as parents are taught a method and are given "homework" in that they are asked to practice the method at home with their children. Scott and Dadds (2009) suggest the use of MI for parents who are either reluctant to engage in the course or who do not follow through on assignments for a variety of reasons. Sometimes we can actually increase resistance in parents by arguing with them about why they need to attend or by persuading or coaxing them to cooperate. This can be done with the best of intentions as we may be worried about the outcome if the parents don't cooperate, particularly if they have been mandated to the class. Using MI helps us to listen to the parents' viewpoints and concerns in a nonjudgmental manner, thus reducing resistance and, it's hoped, increasing motivation to participate in the intervention (Arkowitz, Westra, Miller, & Rollnick, 2008).

WHAT ARE THE LIMITATIONS IN THE USE OF MI?

Currently MI has been applied to clients mostly in the micro (individual) and mezzo (family and group) systems. Besides individual work, there are applications of MI with families (i.e., Gill, Hyde, Shaw, Dishion, & Wilson, 2008) and in group settings (i.e., Santa Ana, Wulfert, & Nietert, 2007; Wagner & Ingersoll, in press). In terms of macro settings, at least two studies have investigated the use of MI to prevent/reduce alcohol and other drug use systemwide across university settings (Miller, Toscova, Miller, & Sanchez, 2000; Newbery, McCambridge, & Strang, 2007), however we don't know much about its use in this area.

One concern that has arisen is that MI methods do not utilize the "person-in-environment" perspective (Northern, 1995) and that using MI takes the focus off of the multiple systems that clients interact with day in and day out. For example, juvenile correctional workers who have participated in MI training have told me that it is one thing to interact with a youthful offender in a manner that helps him or her move toward positive direction. But what if the youth comes from a high-crime area, is illiterate, and has peers who use drugs? How does having motivational conversations help the youth when he or she has to confront all of these other problems? Even using MI methods to help the youth strategize ways to address barriers to, say, school attendance may not be enough to overcome the myriad of problems poor inner-city youth face. In a similar vein, I have heard social workers who work in the field of interpersonal violence (IPV) express concern that MI is "just an individual method" and state that they do not like having the focus on the survivor, instead of on the culture of violence that is perpetuated through our media and music. The person-in-environment perspective has come under criticism, however, in that it is too broad and can be overwhelming for both clients and for us as social workers to address multiple problems across systems (Rogers, 2010). MI can be helpful in setting a specific agenda and goals that can be addressed, and we also need to think of how problems, barriers, and solutions occur for clients within a context.

Another limitation of MI for social work practice may be in the area of learning MI. MI skills are not simple to learn, and research indicates that ongoing supervision, coaching, and feedback of skills are important (Miller, Yahne, Moyers, Martinez, & Pirritano, 2004). It took me quite awhile before I felt my MI skills were good enough to demonstrate an MI interview in front of an audience. Receiving feedback and coaching take time and often are hard to fit into already busy schedules (Forrester et al., 2007; Miller & Mount, 2001). Sometimes agency policy and/or practices are not supportive of the spirit and use of MI (Wahab, 2005a), which again makes learning and practicing MI more of a challenge. Often, though, those who are interested in increasing their MI skills find ways to do so despite time and other constraints (see Chapter 9 for examples).

FINAL THOUGHTS

MI is an evidence-based practice, a communication style based on collaboration, client evocation, and client autonomy support. It fits well with the values of social work but at times is in conflict with current practice, perhaps even more so in settings where clients are involuntary and there is an investment in the outcome. Despite its appeal, it can be challenging to learn, particularly when we are overwhelmed with the demands of our work or work in an agency that does not support a client-centered approach (Miller, Yahne, et al., 2004). Usual methods of communication include asking a lot of questions, perhaps labeling the problem, and seeing ourselves as experts who need to help clients fix their problems. Using MI in many ways means learning how to communicate in a different way. In the next chapter, we will look at where MI came from, what skills are involved with MI, and examine some of the social psychological theories that explain how it works.

2

The Heart
of Motivational Interviewing

In the first chapter we looked at how MI fits well with social work values, ethics, and practice, especially when considering the three aspects of MI spirit: collaboration, evocation, and autonomy support. But where did MI come from? How does one actually implement MI? In other words, what are the skills of MI that might be so different from typical social work interactions? And finally, can we explain how MI works? As we answer these questions, it is hoped that you will have a better understanding of what MI is all about. We will explore MI in more detail in subsequent chapters as we look at how the principles and methods are applied to various social work populations as well as discuss how context may shape how we use MI.

HOW WAS MI DEVELOPED?

Typically new interventions or methods are designed based on utilization of a theory and hypotheses that are then developed and tested (Miller & Rose, 2009). This was not the case in MI. Bill Miller, the creator of MI, describes his work in the 1970s:

I got interested in this field on an internship in Milwaukee. The psychologist-director ... enticed me to work on the alcoholism unit, even though (and because) I had learned nothing about alcoholism. Knowing nothing, I did what came naturally to me—Carl Rogers—and in essence asked patients to teach me about alcoholism and tell me about themselves: how they got to where they were, what they planned to do, etc. I mostly listened with accurate empathy. There was an immediate chemistry—I loved talking to them, and they seemed to enjoy talking to me. Then I began reading about the alleged nature of alcoholics as lying, conniving, defensive, slippery, and incapable of seeing reality. "Gee, these aren't the same patients I've been talking to," I thought. The experience of listening empathically to alcoholics stayed with me and became the basis for motivational interviewing. (in Ashton, 2005, p. 26)

Alcoholism treatment at that time (and to some degree, even today) was based on the thinking that alcoholics were in denial about the seriousness of their drinking and its related problems. In order to break through this denial and to see reality, counselors were encouraged to confront clients about their denial, lying, manipulation, and so on. Once clients had taken the first step of admitting to a problem, and shown motivation to change, then they could begin the recovery process. Clearly Miller's work was at odds with the practice standards at that time and he became more curious as to what, from his experience, seemed to impact clients.

Working at the University of New Mexico, Miller led experimental studies testing behavioral interventions. Several studies included an assessment with brief advice and assignment to a waiting list compared to the same assessment with 10 sessions of cognitive-behavioral individual counseling for clients with problem drinking concerns. The results indicated that both groups did equally as well. Analysis of counselor style used within the assessment found that the clients whose therapists displayed accurate empathy had much better outcomes, even 1 and 2 years later (Miller & Baca, 1983). Miller was also amazed to see that people who were assigned to a self-help control group began to change their own drinking based on just a brief intervention (Miller, 1996). Later, after he began to develop MI, Miller extended this work. People with problem drinking (not labeled as "alcoholics") were recruited to participate in a study called the Drinker's Check-up. Using normative standards of drinking and related physical testing, clients were given feedback regarding where they fell on these various measures. Some were given this information in a client-centered empathic style; others were given the information through a confrontational approach, with the counselors telling the clients that they were "alcoholics." The group that received the confrontation responded with double the amount of resistant statements and only half as much change talk (statements regarding change) as compared to the group that received the empathic counseling style (Miller, Benefield, & Tonigan, 1993).

Soon after his initial work and resulting research findings, Miller went on a sabbatical to Norway and while there met regularly with a training group of psychologists treating alcoholism. During role plays where he demonstrated his counseling methods, the psychologists asked him to specify why he chose certain skills and the decision rules for how he responded to what the client had to say. This forced Miller to think about what had been an unconscious process for him, and he wrote the first conceptual model of MI (Miller, 1983). This model included client-centered work of empathic listening and strategic use of questions and reflections.

In 1989, Miller met Stephen Rollnick, a psychologist from Wales, who had told him that he had been using MI in his work in health care and that it had become very popular in the United Kingdom. He asked to see more written about it. This led to their collaboration on the first book on MI (Miller & Rollnick, 1991) where they provided a more in-depth look at MI, with the focus being on addictions treatment. Rollnick also expanded the concept and importance of ambivalence. A second edition of the book was published in 2002 with a more general focus instead of addictions work, and a third edition is now being written.

As more practitioners and researchers learned about MI, the demand for training in MI increased significantly. In response to the need for proficient trainers, Miller and Rollnick created a process to train trainers, which was the beginning of the MI Network of Trainers, or MINT (Moyers, 2004). Over 2,000 people have completed training for trainers since 1995 (Miller & Rollnick, 2009), thus expanding the potential for learning MI.

WHAT EXACTLY IS INVOLVED WITH MI?

Often, experienced social workers who are taking an introductory workshop in MI tell me that they already know MI as they begin to hear about it. Typically, what they usually mean is that they are familiar with client-centered theory and techniques. Sometimes the social workers or therapists are already using these methods in their practice. Clinicians and others who work using this model tend to embrace the spirit of MI and are anxious to learn more about it. As Miller said, clinicians "recognize" it when they see it and want to learn about it (Miller & Rollnick, 2009).

In Chapter 1 we examined a definition of MI and the three elements of the MI spirit: collaboration, evocation, and autonomy support. As indicated in the history of MI, Miller took elements of Rogers's client-centered theory and work that included accurate empathic listening. Using these methods, Miller worked in a collaborative fashion with alcohol treatment clients and evoked from them their stories, including how they came to be in the treatment center and what their goals were. In reflecting on his work in Norway, he realized that he used questions and reflections to respond to selective statements made by his clients, particularly statements regarding change in the positive direction. This approach was somewhat different from the nondirective nature of Rogers's work (Miller & Rollnick, 2009). Miller's focus on these statements became the basis for what was termed eliciting "self-motivating statements" (Miller, 1983; Miller & Rollnick, 1991) from clients and later changed to eliciting "change talk" (Miller & Rollnick, 2002; Miller & Rose, 2009). How social workers and counselors recognize and address change talk, in many ways, is what makes MI different from the work set forth by Rogers. While MI was initially used in addictions treatment, it has been used and studied in a wide variety of behaviors, as we saw in Chapter 1 (Resnicow et al., 2002).

Beyond implementing the spirit of MI, what else is involved? Although we looked at some of the methods and principles in the first chapter in the section on MI and social work values, I will address them all in depth in the rest of this book. However, a brief overview of the MI principles and skills will provide a better understanding.

The Principles of MI

Before we begin, it is important to remember that we typically use MI with clients regarding changing a specific behavior. This behavior might be identified by clients themselves or by someone else, such as spouse or child welfare social worker who has referred a client to, say, a mental health agency (Moyers & Rollnick, 2002). We may not always have a target behavior. Say a client wants to discuss whether to move out of state or not. Either choice has positive outcomes for the client. In this case we have "equipoise," which is no specific goal or direction in mind (Rollnick et al., 2008). MI spirit and skills can still be utilized but with no need to focus on a direction. Also, in MI the process is usually on one of two phases: in Phase 1, we work toward building motivation to change, and in Phase 2, we work with clients regarding making a commitment and plan for change.

There are four principles in MI (Miller & Rollnick, 2002). The first one is to *express empathy*. This is done through accurate empathy whereby the client experiences acceptance and knows that we understand their perspective on the concern or behavior under discussion. This is different from *agreeing* with clients. Accurate empathy is achieved through reflective listening. As we listen and reflect back to our clients, we learn, for instance, the reasons a client leaves her children home alone so that she can go socialize at the local bar. We listen carefully to the client's thoughts on this as well as to what other values and ideas she possesses regarding parenting. As we reflect them back to her in a nonjudgmental manner, the client feels accepted and valued, which may make her more willing to look at aspects of this behavior that she finds uncomfortable.

The second principle is to *develop discrepancy*. As our clients engage with us through the expression of empathy, we learn about their motivators or the goals and values that they hold deeply. Either through their discussion or the strategic reflections we use, clients begin to examine the conflict or discrepancy between the behavior and the values they hold. We confront clients, not in a negative or shaming way, but by holding up a mirror to examine the ambivalence they may be experiencing: as in the above example, the client may state that she likes being around other adults in the bar, and she realizes that leaving her children alone does not fit with her desire to be a good mother. The goal in MI is to have the client state the reasons or need for change (Miller & Rollnick, 2002).

The third principle is to *roll with resistance*. Miller and Rollnick (2002) have framed resistance somewhat differently than those promoting other types of therapy models (Engle & Arkowitz, 2006). Clients, particularly those who are mandated to receive our services, often begin with what is called "sustain talk," or discussion of why they can't, won't, shouldn't, or don't need to change a behavior. Frustrated, we often try to convince clients otherwise by providing information, trying to convince, and sometimes, warning or threatening. Resistance comes out of our attempts to change clients' minds and is seen when clients "push back" by arguing, interrupting, changing the subject, or even offering passive compliance (Rosengren, 2009). One metaphor used in MI is that we end up "wrestling" with clients instead of "dancing" with them. Clients who are resistant are signaling to us that something in our interaction needs to be different (Moyers & Rollnick, 2002). If we roll with the resistance, the energy goes out of the exchange, and clients are less likely to be on the defensive. Instead of arguing back, we reflect their thoughts in order to understand their position. Again, we are not agreeing with our clients but are attempting to take the energy out of the resistance by not making the case why they should or must make the change.

The fourth principle is to *support self-efficacy*. Self-efficacy is the belief in oneself to achieve a certain behavior or outcome (Bandura, 1999). We serve as coaches or cheerleaders for our clients, providing hope and confidence that can come from affirming client strengths or past successes. The belief that change can be achieved is critical for clients who have little confidence in themselves. Miller and Rollnick (2002) also indicate that along with supporting self-efficacy we remind our clients that the decision for change is ultimately up to them. We can act as a resource and support for our clients, but they are the ones who must make the decision as to if and how to change.

The Skills of MI

Miller and Rollnick (2002) call client-centered skills the fundamental strategies that are used to engage the client and allow us as social workers to begin to understand their perspectives on the situation or concern. These skills are open-ended questions, affirmations, reflections, and summaries, often referred to by the acronym OARS. *Open-ended questions* are those that have a variety of possible answers and do not limit the client. Asking our clients, "What is on your mind today?" or "How would you like to use this time together?" allows them the opportunity to set the agenda of what they would like to cover. Of course, you as the social worker or probation officer, for instance, may also have items or topics that you would like to cover and in working in a collaborative fashion, you share with the client your agenda items as well.

Affirmations are statements we make about an attribute or characteristic or even a past behavior that was supportive of client change. An example would be, "You are a real survivor and when you put your mind to something, you do it, despite the circumstances that are thrown at you." Typically affirmations start with "You ... " with an emphasis on who the client is or what the client has done. Telling a client, "I am proud of you" implies a value statement and keeps the focus on the social worker.

Reflective statements or *reflections* are statements the social worker makes that repeat, rephrase, or paraphrase what the client has said. These are called simple reflections. Reflections can also be more complex in that we may use different words to describe what we think the client means. Reflections can also "continue the paragraph" in that we might have a hypothesis about where the client is going next and check this out through a reflective statement (Miller & Rollnick, 2002). For example, a mother may be describing how difficult it is to care for her adult daughter who is ill with a terminal disease. She tells her social worker, "I want to help her, but sometimes I am just too frail myself and can't do the physical lifting that she needs." The social worker, in continuing the paragraph, may reflect, "You are wondering if now is the time to see about getting some help." Reflections can also be double-sided where the social worker reflects the ambivalence that the client is struggling with: "On the one hand, it has been important for you to take care of her yourself since you love her so, and on the other hand, you are feeling overwhelmed and tired with all that you have to do."

Double-sided reflections are important because they help our clients hear their ambivalence. The goal of MI is to work toward resolving ambivalence in the direction of change (Miller & Rollnick, 2002). Often clients are stuck on the fence of ambivalence, wanting to change and yet not wanting to change at the same time. For instance, a client struggling with bipolar disorder may hate the feelings that medications give him, and yet he wants to succeed at holding a job and maintaining an intimate relationship. Strategic use of OARS skills and reflections that provide both sides of the ambivalent thoughts or behaviors can help our clients become unstuck.

Summaries are important in MI because we use them to pull together the various statements that clients have made and perhaps even link these statements to something they previously discussed. Summaries can be formulated in a strategic manner and serve to show clients that we are listening as well as to help to make connections for clients. In the scenario of the social worker with the older adult client, perhaps the social worker might say, "So let me see if I have everything you described: You have been taking care of your daughter now for a long time on your own, and as her condition worsens, you find you are having trouble lifting her and helping her to the restroom. You are able to help her with eating, but even that is getting more difficult. You have been struggling with a decision as to whether to get help because you feel as a mother, and because you love her, you should do it all. A part of you feels like you are letting her down by asking for help, and another part of you knows that this isn't true and that you can only do so much. If you were to get help, it would have to be affordable and be from someone who is kind to your daughter." In this instance, the social worker summarized what the client was experiencing, including her concerns for herself. She linked them to what the client had indicated would be important if she were to get help, all the while conveying the idea that she (the social worker) understood how important the client's love for her daughter was.

Sometimes before we provide a summary we can *elicit change talk*. Change talk is one aspect that makes MI unique from client-centered models. In MI, we listen acutely for statements that clients make about their desire, ability, reasons, or need for change. In the above scenario, the mother has said she couldn't do the caregiving alone anymore (ability, or lack of ability in this case) and felt frail herself (reason). Perhaps if the social worker had next asked, "If you were to get help, what kind of help would you want?" the client might then have indicated that she thought maybe she needed help that was affordable and wanted it to be from a person who was kind (desire). As we hear change talk in the direction of change, we reinforce it by reflecting, affirming, or asking for an elaboration: "What would a person who is kind to your daughter be like?" As the social worker reflects back the answers the client gives, she is demonstrating empathy to the client that she hears how important this trait is. This helps to reduce the client's ambivalence about bringing a stranger into her home to help her with her daughter.

In MI, we show collaboration first by asking what clients know about or have tried regarding the behavior under discussion, "What do you know about caregiving agencies?" and then by *asking permission* before we provide advice or information. The social worker asks the client if she would be interested in hearing about some options for finding a good caregiver and may provide her with some resources. Finally, if appropriate, the social worker *asks for a commitment* from the client by asking her what she will do next or if she is willing to call some of the agencies that she listed. This can be the *plan* that the client decides she will follow.

WHAT MAKES MI WORK?

Most of us learned in college or graduate school that theories should be used as the basis for any development of an intervention strategy. We need to be able to explain why something should work based on logical hypotheses. The development of MI took a slightly different path, as mentioned earlier. Bill Miller, though trained as a behavioral psychologist, used the work of Carl Rogers to inform his interactions with clients with alcohol problems. However, he based his methods on what he saw was working—responding to various types of clients' speech in an empathic manner. He developed MI from mostly an atheoretical position, so he began to explore what some of the theoretical bases might be to what he was already practicing (Miller & Rose, 2009). Others have drawn links to other social psychology theories that seem to explain what makes MI work (Britton, Williams, & Conner, 2008; Leffingwell, Neumann, Babitze, Leedy, & Walters, 2007; Markland, Ryan, Tobin, & Rollnick, 2005; Moyers & Rollnick, 2002; Vansteenkiste & Sheldon, 2006). Only recently have I added material into my MI training/ classroom work about these theories, for other than Rogers's client-centered theory, social workers typically do not study them (Payne, 2005). Even though students' eyes tend to glaze over at the mere mention of the word "theory," I have found that understanding these theories has really made MI come alive for me and has impacted how I teach it. Understanding why MI works the way it does provides the foundation for the skills we utilize (Moyers, 2004).

As social workers, it is important that we ask ourselves from time to time about our view of human nature. Most social workers are attracted to the field for humanistic reasons, such as altruism: They want to make a difference, they are concerned about social justice, and so on (LeCroy, 2002). We believe that given the right conditions, whether in the micro, mezzo, or macro environments, people can make changes and overcome obstacles. Sometimes this perspective can erode owing to day-to-day work that might include problems with supervisors, rules, regulations, and lack of resources, or even problems with our clients. As the idealism we had when we left school with diploma in hand begins to wane, often it impacts our perspectives on our clients and maybe even how we interact with them. As we review the following theories, please think about your own perspectives and how these theories are similar to or different from your past and/ or current views of human nature.

Client-Centered Theory

Rogers's client-centered theory was based on a humanistic model of human nature. In brief, he believed that all humans strive toward health or positive growth. Clients are seen as being experts on their lives who understand best the reasons and contexts for engaging in certain behaviors, even those that are problematic (Rogers, 1957). Miller (1983) captured this notion in his early description of MI when he said, "A motivational interviewing approach treats the individual as a responsible adult, capable of making responsible decisions and coming to the right solutions" (p. 155). It makes sense then, that in MI we work in a collaborative fashion to evoke from clients their perspective, using reflections to gain and demonstrate understanding. Rogers advocated being nondirective with clients and held that practitioners should follow the lead of the client. MI is different from Rogers's theory/model in that there is usually a specific direction or goal for behavioral change that the social worker or therapist works toward (Miller & Rose, 2009) and we can use our questions, reflections, and summaries strategically to work in a particular direction. Although we support clients' autonomy to make decisions, even those we may not necessarily agree with, we still may have a specific behavioral goal in our interviews with clients. Client-centered theory is related to the MI principle of express empathy and the spirit aspect of collaboration.

Dissonance Theory

If humans are striving toward health, as indicated in client-centered theory, then humans hold values at some level that are consistent with health or growth. This might, depending on culture, include values such as wanting to be a good parent, be healthy, loved, admired, productive, and the like. Often we engage in behaviors that are in conflict with these values (e.g., smoking, gossiping, nagging our children, overeating). According to Festinger (1957), people experience cognitive dissonance when they engage in behaviors that are in conflict with internalized values. An example would be someone who values health but still smokes. This conflict produces anxiety or tension that can cause people to either (1) change the behavior, (2) rationalize or justify the behavior, or (3) tell oneself that the particular value is not that important. The smoker in this example could quit smoking, tell himself that he only smokes six cigarettes a day which aren't that much, or think that since he has other health issues, being healthy is not that important to him. This theory was initially included in Miller's first conception of MI (1983), and he proposed that the role of the practitioner was to increase dissonance through empathic but strategic reflections, relating the behavior to the value. The goal is to work toward changed behavior, rather than changed attitude or values. All of this is to be done without shaming, negative confronting, or reducing the client's self-efficacy to change. This is what led to the MI principle of develop discrepancy.

Self-Determination Theory

Self-determination theory is also based on a humanistic model (Vansteenkiste & Sheldon, 2006). In this theory, humans strive toward positive growth and tend to do so in situations that support their autonomy, competence, and relatedness to others (Ryan & Deci, 2002). These three needs are universal across cultures. According to the authors of this theory, we humans have intrinsic motivations, and when we are intrinsically motivated, we choose to engage in activities because we find them enjoyable. We can also be extrinsically motivated. We go to work not so much for the enjoyment but for some other reward such as income. (Hopefully, we have some enjoyment in it too!) We can also be motivated to participate in activities because we are pretty much forced to, such as attending traffic school. For activities that require extrinsic motivation, such as work, the more the setting supports our autonomy, competency, and relatedness needs, the more likely we are to thrive in those settings (Gagne & Deci, 2005). Thus, particularly in settings with mandated clients, those clients who can have their autonomy, competency, and relatedness needs met, as much as possible, will be more likely to engage in the services that are provided. In MI we support autonomy by asking clients for their perceptions and solutions and by affirming that they ultimately are the ones who must make decisions and choices. We support competence by working with clients to come up with their own solutions or by asking permission before we give advice or information. Relatedness comes from the use of reflections and summaries that are given in an empathic manner and the collaborative nature of our interactions with clients (Markland et al., 2005). Self-determination theory is related to the MI spirit concept of autonomy support.

Self-Perception Theory

According to self-perception theory, people perceive themselves as they articulate their thoughts in social interactions (Bem, 1972). Thus, how clients talk about problems can be very important. If clients use a lot of sustain talk, then they may be more likely to perceive themselves as unable or unwilling to change because they become more closely identified with or committed to the behavior. If clients engage in change talk, then they may begin to think of themselves in a different way. Through our empathetic reflections, with the use of summaries and questions where clients are asked to elaborate, clients can "hear" themselves and develop a different perspective on their situation (Cain, 2007). Recently at a workshop I led, a social worker who participated in an MI learning exercise that involved discussing her own reasons for change, stated, "I came up with reasons [for change] that I didn't even know I had! Having to say them out loud really made me think!" This is related to the MI spirit concept of evocation.

Self-Affirmation Theory

Self-affirmation theory states that people need to perceive themselves as competent in order to protect their self-worth, or literally, their "self" (Steele, 1988). If self-worth is kept intact, people are able to hear messages that are uncomfortable (Reed & Aspinwall, 1998). When clients feel that their self-worth is under attack, they may react by becoming resistant. Thus, an important aspect of MI is to avoid labeling a client (as drug addict, drunk driver, bipolar, borderline, neglectful mother, etc.), for this threatens the self-worth, is stigmatizing, and can cause clients to react negatively. Affirming clients' strengths, characteristics, and capabilities demonstrates that we recognize them and may help clients become more open to discussing areas of concern. This is related to the MI principle of express empathy and to the spirit aspect of collaboration.

Self-Efficacy Theory

In a similar vein, self-efficacy theory is related to people's perceptions or appraisals of their ability to engage in or perform a particular behavior (Bandura, 1994, 1999). People with high self-efficacy have strong beliefs that they are able to accomplish challenging goals. Those with low self-efficacy tend to avoid tasks in which they fear they will fail. In MI, motivation to change has two aspects: the importance of the change and the confidence to make the change (Rollnick, Miller, & Butler, 2008). Clients may give high importance to making a change such as quitting smoking and also feel low in confidence to actually do it. According to Bandura (1994), efficacy can be influenced in four ways, and they are listed in sequence according to their strength in raising self-efficacy: (1) through accomplishment of other, similar experiences; (2) through observing someone similar achieve the change or task (modeling); (3) through persuasion by someone else that change is possible, and (4) through reduction of stress or negative mood state toward the change.

How can we support self-efficacy, using this knowledge? Affirmations can have a strong role. Thus thinking about affirmations from an MI perspective (and the deficit vs. competency perspective), the goal of the affirmation is not to let the client know what we think or value (i.e., "I think you are a devoted daughter" or "It is good you chose to take care of your dad") but to let the client know that we see what they already see in themselves (i.e., "You worked hard to make sure everything was taken care of for your father"). We first comment on clients' own past accomplishments and abilities. If clients ask for advice on how to change, we can describe what other clients have done in similar situations (modeling). In MI we try to avoid persuasion as this tends to cause resistance, but we can help reduce stress through helping clients pick small, obtainable strategies when they are ready to change (Rosengren, 2009)

Ambivalence, a key concept is MI, is often the product of clients not knowing if they could change, or even if they wanted to. Leffingwell and colleagues (2007) indicate that self-efficacy theory and self-affirmation theory can lead us to assume it is better to recognize and discuss client strengths/abilities/characteristics before proceeding to bring up subjects that may be more negatively charged for a client. Clients may be more open to exploring their ambivalence or the "downside" of a behavior when they feel they are not being judged as a person.

Psychological Reactance Theory

According to Brehm and Brehm (1981), psychological reactance occurs when people react to preserve their autonomy. Thus, when people think that their free will or choice is being threatened, they react by becoming angry, state the opposite side of the argument, or choose to continue the behavior under discussion. Thus, a parent court-ordered to a parenting class may choose to attend in order to keep her children, but in the classroom she is disruptive or uninvolved. This can be her way of asserting her autonomy and according to reactance theory, is *normal* behavior when someone is in a forced situation. MI takes reactance theory a bit further by indicating that resistance (or reactance) comes from the interaction between the client and the social worker or therapist. This supports another principle, to roll with resistance, because the resistance is something we (or the context of the situation, as described above) are doing that is causing the client to react negatively. Of course, we can't change a court order to attend parenting class, but we can use MI skills to work with resistance that isn't even of our own creation.

FINAL THOUGHTS

So to sum up, in combining these theories, we see that clients have a need for connection, competence, and autonomy (self-determination theory) and when this autonomy or self-worth is threatened (reactance theory and self-affirmation theory), clients tend to react in a way to preserve these things (sustain talk and/or resistance). They listen to themselves describe why they can't or won't change or they reduce the importance of the problem (self-perception theory, discrepancy theory). Clients who feel engaged, valued, and connected to their social worker (client-centered theory) are more likely to see themselves as competent and capable (self-efficacy theory, self-perception theory) and become more open to discussing reasons and need for change (change talk). And research tells us that the more clients talk about change, the more likely they are to embark on this change (Amrhein, Miller, Yahne, Paler, & Fulcher, 2003; Apodaca & Longabaugh, 2009).

In MI, we use strategic open-ended questions, affirmations, reflections, and summaries to guide our clients in a particular direction, working to highlight and affirm change talk and decrease the use of sustain talk. We help them examine their ambivalence and begin to resolve it in the direction of positive change. We roll with resistance that arises when clients have felt their autonomy or self-worth threatened and either reflect their concerns or change our strategies. As MI practitioners, we work to evoke their thoughts and ideas regarding the problem and solutions. We affirm clients' strengths and provide hope for change, all the while supporting their autonomy to make these changes.

In the following chapters we examine more closely the principles and skills of MI, put them in contexts that are common to social workers, and provide sample interviews. Hopefully having an understanding of the history and theories that support why MI works as well as it does will be helpful as you learn and practice MI skills.

3

Motivational Interviewing and the Engagement and Assessment Process

WITH HILDA LOUGHRAN AND SALLY MATHIESEN

Not only do social workers love to talk, we love to ask questions. Often we enter this field for altruistic reasons regarding social justice but also because we like people and are innately curious about their lives. We wonder about how our clients came to be in their current situation. We may be interested to know how their background, environment, and family history shaped and influenced who they are today. We are curious about what they are going to be like to work with and what they expect from us and our agency. All of these questions are in our heads when we prepare to meet with clients for the first time.

Miller and Rollnick (2002) emphasize elicitation or the drawing out from the client as an important ingredient in the spirit of MI. Well, this is easy enough for curious social workers! How do we take our interest in people and use it in an MI-adherent manner to learn about our clients? How can MI help facilitate the engagement and assessment process? We are good at asking questions; what other strategies can we use to evoke thoughts, ideas, and concerns from our clients? How does the context of our interactions with clients make a difference? What exactly do we want to elicit? As we begin to examine and answer these questions, please keep in mind that we use MI skills and strategies with a focus on behavior change. Many times, the initial behavior change target that we have in our minds is to engage clients in services. We want to help them resolve their ambivalence about working with us and using the other services our agencies or programs have to offer. Sometimes our enthusiasm for change gets in the way of this and we move on to discussing change before clients are ready for it. In MI, engagement and assessment are best understood as interwoven processes.

Typically the first contact with clients—and maybe the only contact we have—involves both engagement and assessment, which are traditionally linked together in social work practice (Kirst-Ashman & Hull, 2008). We work to quickly establish rapport with clients, put them at ease, and determine what their needs and concerns are. Social work literature on this topic encourages us to work in a collaborative fashion with clients, actively soliciting clients' perspectives, using active listening and the strengths perspective, to determine a mutually agreed-upon conception of the problems and goals (Boyle, Hull, Mather, Smith, & Farley, 2008; Compton, Galaway, & Cournoyer, 2005; Kirst-Ashman & Hull, 2008).

The MI spirit and skills blend well with the social work understanding of engagement and assessment and can facilitate this process (Carroll et al., 2006; Swartz et al., 2007). We use OARS skills to engage, build rapport, and learn of clients' concerns. Using MI challenges us to think about how we do this, what information we want to gather, and how the strategic use of MI skills can be utilized. With MI, we take our curiosity and use it in a client-centered and guiding manner.

Of course, engagement and assessment may also need to cover the needs of the agency and will be impacted by the context of the interview. The type of information that is gathered may be brief, in-depth, and/or focus on a particular area, such as prior mental health treatment and medication usage. As we look at engagement and assessment, it is important to think about exactly what we do—and do not—need to know and how we will use the information that is gathered. We might gather information that is interesting to us but has little relevance to clients' concerns.

It is also useful to consider the quality of the information we gather through the assessment process. Here is where the links between engagement and assessment are important. The process of engagement begins possibly even before the first interview. Clients may formulate ideas about what to expect from the interview based on previous experiences, the way the interview is organized, and how they are approached by their social worker. If those preconceived ideas are positive, then the engagement process may be accelerated and of course the opposite may also be true. We may have to counteract negative ideas on the part of clients before any progress on engagement can be made. A commitment to the spirit of MI will address any preconceived negativity so that it does not interfere with the respectful and affirming stance to work effectively with clients.

Engagement then is an interactive dance with our clients. While pursuing the information that will assist in developing a thorough assessment, we may be tested by some clients. Sometimes clients give snippets of information to start just to check out our responses. Utilizing our skills in listening and reflecting will encourage clients to engage in disclosure of information that will lead to quality assessments. This too is an interactive process since getting important and pertinent information in the assessment allows us to be more accurate in our empathizing with clients and further enhance the engagement process.

Written assessment measures and client needs assessment tools can be an important part of an MI interview. Sometimes written measures that clients fill out provide information that might not come up in an in-person interview (Hohman, Roads, & Corbett, 2010). For instance, Miller and Brown (1994) created the 69-item "What I Want from Treatment" scale for clients entering substance use treatment (see *casaa.unm.edu/inst/ What%20I%20Want%20From%20Treatment.pdf*), with items ranging from "I would like to learn how to have fun without using drugs" to "I would like to discuss having been physically abused." Clients can use this form to indicate whether or not these areas are important for them to address while working with a counselor or program. Likewise, clients may also receive feedback regarding scores on an assessment tool, such as from an alcohol use measure, and be asked for their thoughts on the information (Babor, McRee, Kassebaum, Grimaldi, & Bray, 2007).

When the engagement/assessment dance is underway, it is possible to build on these processes by employing MI elicitation strategies. Elicitation can include:

- Learning what our clients want out of the interview.
- How they came to be talking with us at this time and in this place.
- Their perspectives on their concerns and goals for change.
- Their responses to written assessment measures that may be reviewed.
- Their ambivalence about change.
- Their values, strengths, attributes, and prior successful change experiences that might aid them in the change process.

- Their ideas of how to go about making a change or addressing their concerns.
- Their knowledge about resources or steps in the direction of change.
- Barriers or environmental difficulties that may get in the way of change.
- Initial steps toward planning (Boyle et al., 2008; Compton, Galloway, & Courmoyer, 2005; Swartz et al., 2007).

ELICITATION FROM A CLIENT PERSPECTIVE

Working with a social worker at first may be intimidating or even frightening to clients based on the situation and context. Clients may be reluctant to open up and verbalize what their concerns or needs are or may feel embarrassed or angry about their situation. Bradshaw (1972), differentiated between normative, felt, and expressed needs. Normative needs of clients are those determined by experts. Using our professional knowledge and experience, and maybe even our measurement procedures, we determine what clients need or should need. Felt needs are those that clients may feel but are reluctant, for whatever reason, to express. Expressed needs are those needs that clients state they have for service provision. Clients may ask for help based on what they think the agency offers but not on what they feel they need. Other times they may feel overwhelmed by their problems and want their social worker to provide them with direction and answers. Clients may not wish to state their concerns due to fears of losing child custody or possible legal problems. They may be hesitant to disclose problems to their social worker who may be of a different race or class, due to previous negative interactions or even discrimination (Elliott, Bjelajac, Fallot, Markoff, & Reed, 2005; Hohman, Roads, & Corbett, 2010; Swartz et al., 2007). If we want to truly find out what is of concern to our clients, we need to move away from a focus on normative or expert-decided needs and set the stage for evoking felt and expressed needs.

Using an MI approach can help alleviate fears or resistance as we use the spirit of MI to help form an alliance with our clients. This alliance, or engagement, is based on empathy, collaboration, and nonjudgmental acceptance. Using OARS skills, the social worker utilizes open-ended questions but mainly uses reflective listening skills to draw out clients. As Compton and colleagues (2005, p. 194) write, "It is better to listen than to question." The more empathic we are, the more likely our clients will be willing to open up to us and disclose their expressed needs (Moyers, Miller, & Hendrickson, 2005). Also, using reflective listening skills takes us away from the "question–answer trap," which blocks communication (Miller & Rollnick, 2002). This trap occurs when we take the lead in the conversation and ask question after question with our clients, thus limiting their opportunities to discuss what is on their minds.

ELICITATION? WELL, MAYBE . . .

For some social workers, thinking about this type of an engagement and assessment process may be a practice paradigm shift. We are good at asking questions (Boyle et al., 2008) and trying to figure out, from our expert knowledge and experience, what exactly the issues and problems are. Working in a collaborative instead of expert manner may be a transition for those who are used to utilizing a medical model (diagnose and treat) or who are in dual roles where social workers must also serve child safety (CPS) or society (probation).

Despite the profession's desire to have engagement and assessment be collaborative, sometimes the clients' perspectives of clients are not taken into consideration (Slade, Phelan, Thornicraft, & Parkman, 1996). Turnell, who has worked extensively in child welfare services, writes, "One of the greatest problems to bedevil child protection practice is that assessment and planning processes privilege the professional voice and erase the perspectives of children, parents, and other family members" (Turnell, 2010). The perspectives of the professional may be given more credence than those of clients based on the type of services or treatment that is being offered. Clients who abuse substances, experience mental illness, neglect their children, or commit crimes may be seen as having limited insight into their problems and thus unable or incapable of making good decisions (Walker, Logan, Clark, & Leukefeld, 2005).

As we think about how to engage and assess clients utilizing an MI approach, an important question becomes, *How privileged is our professional voice?* Whose opinion and viewpoint is most important in our agency setting? How will we be changing practice as we seek to privilege both client and professional voices? Elicitation goes beyond asking questions; how we interact with clients is done with the recognition that clients are the experts on their own lives. The collaboration comes from utilizing our knowledge along with that of our clients and in the guiding process as we focus on and negotiate an area of change. Working with clients to help them verbalize feelings and needs that they may not have disclosed before is a very responsible task. On the one hand it involves using the appropriate skills to facilitate clients in revealing new information about themselves, their hopes, feelings, and "felt" needs, while on the other hand we must take care to keep the discussion realistic and grounded.

Although agencies or funders may dictate what is gathered in assessment interviews, an MI interview starts with brief engagement through the use of OARS and then utilizes agenda setting to see what exactly clients want to discuss. We may have a specific area we need to cover, but our clients may want to talk to us about something entirely different. At this point we can negotiate agendas with clients that meet both of our needs. For instance, a client coming to a domestic violence shelter for help may be more interested in getting information about how she can be tested for a sexually transmitted disease than in describing her experiences with inter-personal violence. Using MI, we can ask the client what she wants to discuss as well as describe to her the areas we need to cover. Agenda setting is a collaborative process that works to engage clients as well as support their needs for autonomy.

Besides eliciting what clients want to discuss and their thoughts or ideas about problems, in MI we can ask clients about the *knowledge* they have about the concern, problem, or remedy under discussion. This is so that we can understand what they know and honor before we rush in to provide explanations. It is also a way to evoke what it is they want to know or need more information about (Rollnick, Miller, & Butler, 2008). In MI, this is called *elicit–provide–elicit,* or EPE. First we elicit or ask what the client already knows about the topic. Next we provide, with permission, information or feedback. We follow this up with another eliciting question, asking clients what they think of this or what other information they might need to know. When providing information, Rollnick et al. (2008) remind us to be careful of the *righting reflex*, which is when we want to advise, warn, or fix problems for the client. This can often occur when we are giving information or discussing problems. Most likely our clients have already thought about ways to address their concerns that work best for them in the context of their lives.

THE MI "ASSESSMENT SANDWICH"

One method for integrating an assessment process within an MI interview is to use the MI "assessment sandwich" (Martino et al., 2006). In this model, the first 20 minutes of an intake/assessment interview is focused on using OARS skills to engage and build rapport with clients and gain their perspectives on this concerns or problems. The middle part of the interview is dedicated to conducting the standard agency protocol for assessment and to providing feedback or discussion on any assessment tools that clients may have filled out, again using MI skills including summaries. The final 20 minutes of the interview is to use MI skills to elicit ideas about change and to begin the process of planning.

ELICITATION IN THE ENGAGEMENT AND ASSESSMENT PROCESS: EXAMPLE AND DIALOGUE

The following vignette is about a client with serious mental illness and alcohol use problems (co-occurring disorder), and the dialogue demonstrates the use of MI in the engagement and assessment process. In this interview, the target behavior is to engage the client, Robert, in services as well as to learn about his concerns, which will help begin the process of intervention/treatment planning. The social worker incorporates the use of the Camberwell Assessment of Need Short Appraisal Schedule—Patient Rated (CANSAS-P—Phelan et al., 1995; Slade, Thornicroft, Loftus, Phelan, & Wykes, 1999; Trauer, Tobias, & Slade, 2008), a validated needs assessment instrument for clients receiving mental health services. This measure lists 22 areas of possible need for service (i.e, housing, self-care, physical health, alcohol, among others). Clients are asked to rate each need as no need, met need, unmet need, or don't want to answer. Those needs that were designated as unmet needs can be assessed in further detail in later interviews. See Figure 3.1 for an example of a completed form. Information from this needs assessment tool is incorporated into the following MI assessment interview to help demonstrate how to utilize a standardized measure to elicit client concerns.

It should also be noted that some modifications of MI are recommended when it is used with clients with serious mental illness/psychotic disorders. The modifications include using simple open questions and reflections, presenting frequent affirmations and summaries, pausing and giving time for responses, and avoiding reflections of "disturbing or despairing statements" as they can create more hopelessness for clients (Carey, Leontieva, Dimmock, Maisto, & Batki, 2007; Martino, Carroll, Kostas, Perkins, & Rounsaville, 2002, pp. 301, 304). Simple reflections and summaries may help clients be more cognitively organized and stay on track (Martino, 2007).

Name: *Robert*
Other identifying information (e.g., date of birth):
Date of completion:

Instructions: Please tick one box in each row (22 in total).

No need = This area is not a serious problem for me at all.
Met need = This area is not a serious problem for me because of help I am given.
Unmet need = This area remains a serious problem for me despite any help I am given.

	No need	Met need	Unmet need	I don't want to answer
1. Accommodation *What kind of place do you live in?*	☐	☐	☑	○
2. Food *Do you get enough to eat?*	☑	☐	☐	○
3. Looking after the home *Are you able to look after your home?*	☑	☐	☐	○
4. Self-care *Do you have problems keeping clean and tidy?*	☑	☐	☐	○
5. Daytime activities *How do you spend your day?*	☐	☐	☑	○
6. Physical health *How well do you feel physically?*	☑	☐	☐	○
7. Psychotic symptoms *Do you ever hear voices or have problems with your thoughts?*	☐	☑	☐	○
8. Information on condition and treatment *Have you been given clear information about your medication?*	☐	☐	☑	○
9. Psychological distress *Have you recently felt very sad or low?*	☐	☐	☑	○
10. Safety to self *Do you ever have thoughts of harming yourself?*	☑	☐	☐	○
11. Safety to others *Do you think you could be a danger to other people's safety?*	☑	☐	☐	○
12. Alcohol *Does drinking cause you any problems?*	☐	☐	☑	○
13. Drugs *Do you take any drugs that aren't prescribed?*	☑	☐	☐	○

(continued)

	No need	Met need	Unmet need	I don't want to answer
14. Company *Are you happy with your social life?*	☐	☐	☑	○
15. Intimate relationships *Do you have a partner?*	☐	☐	☐	☒
16. Sexual expression *How is your sex life?*	☐	☐	☐	☒
17. Child care *Do you have any children under 18?*	☑	☐	☐	○
18. Basic education *Any difficulty in reading, writing or understanding English.*	☑	☐	☐	○
19. Telephone *Do you know how to use a telephone?*	☑	☐	☐	○
20. Transport *How do you find using the bus, tram, or train?*	☑	☐	☐	○
21. Money *How do you find budgeting your money?*	☐	☐	☑	○
22. Benefits *Are you getting all the money you are entitled to?*	☐	☐	☑	○

Many thanks for completing the CANSAS-P.

FIGURE 3.1. Self-rated version of the Camberwell Assessment of Need. Copyright 2007 by the Royal College of Psychiatrists. All rights reserved. The adult CAN was developed by Mike Slade, Graham Thornicroft, and others at the Health Service and Population Research Department, Institute of Psychiatry, King's College London. The CANSAS-P was adapted from the adult CAN by Mike Slade and evaluated by Glen Tobias and Tom Trauer. Further information from *www.iop. kcl.ac.uk/prism/can.*

Clients with co-occurring disorders often have multiple life problems, and it is the task of the interviewer to increase motivation in a number of areas, particularly treatment engagement and medication adherence (Martino & Moyers, 2008).

Our client in this scenario, Robert, is a 38-year-old Hispanic single male with a long history of psychotic symptoms and hospitalizations. Currently homeless, he was living in a board and care facility in the downtown area of a large city until 3 months ago and had recently begun a volunteer position as a clerk at a large garden store. An angry verbal dispute with his roommate resulted in Robert leaving the board and care, living on the streets, and not using any psychiatric medications. He also had a verbal dispute at his job and was asked to leave. Robert states that he drinks when he has the money to buy liquor, but he has cut back the amount that he drinks since he left his most recent residence. He denies using other drugs. A local assertive community treatment[1] (ACT) outreach team contacted Robert, and he agreed to seek services. His goals are to have his own apartment and to live as independently as possible, but he continues to experience troubled relationships with family and roommates.

Currently, Robert presents primarily with negative symptoms, including flat affect, diminished interest, and diminished social drive. He denies any suicidal or homicidal ideation at this time. He has repeatedly exhibited behaviors consistent with those labeled schizophrenia, paranoid type. He was interviewed one week after the first contact with ACT and is using their Welcoming Services (including laundry, shower, and groups). The setting for the interview is an agency that provides these welcoming services and other outpatient services.

Robert presents as polite and cooperative with the interviewer. He is relatively well groomed, with long, clean hair and clean, casual clothes. He makes little eye contact and sits with his arms crossed over his chest during the interview. His speech is monotone, a bit pressured and garbled at times. He filled out the CANSAS-P form during an earlier intake interview as well as answered standard risk-assessment questions regarding suicidal/homicidal thinking. Not every item in the CANSAS-P is covered in this dialogue owing to the need for brevity.

Please note that the following coding system, based on the Motivational Interviewing Treatment Integrity (MITI; Moyers, Martin, Manuel, Miller, & Ernst, 2010), will be used for all dialogues in this book.

- GI = giving information
- SR = simple reflection
- CR = complex reflection
- OQ = open-ended question
- CQ = closed-ended question

- MIA = MI adherent (affirming, asking permission, emphasizing personal control, support)

---

[1]ACT is a program for those with serious mental illness that includes individual treatment, rehabilitation, and support by a multidisciplinary team in an intense manner in a community setting (Boust, Kuhns, & Studer, 2005).

SOCIAL WORKER: Hey Robert, my name is Susie Maxwell and I am a social worker here at Horizon House. I understand that you met with some people here and learned a little bit about our services [GI].

CLIENT: The shower, I used the shower.

SOCIAL WORKER: You were able to use the shower [SR].

CLIENT: Yeah, that was good.

SOCIAL WORKER: You were happy with that [SR].

CLIENT: The people here were pretty nice. I don't know how much I want to go to all that group stuff. I've done that. I just wanna have my own space. I've had roommates, I know it's a lot of my fault, I mean I don't like living with other people. I just stay away.

SOCIAL WORKER: Some of the things that you found here were that you liked the shower facilities and the staff was pretty nice. You're concerned with what else might be involved with being here [CR].

CLIENT: I'm thinking that you all might start pushing me—what about meds, what about drinking, what about drug use—and I have done this. I have been in this for a long time. So, I just don't want you to push me. I know what I need.

SOCIAL WORKER: Well, my job is not to push you but to get to know you [GI]. But this is your time [MIA—emphasizing personal control] and I am curious as to how you might like to use it. Typically we use it to find out more about you as a person, things you're good at, things you like to do, and also some things that you are concerned about, where we might be able to help you [GI]. So I am curious as to how you would like to use this time together [OQ]?

CLIENT: I'm not sure, not sure. Can you understand me OK? I've been told that I'm hard to understand.

SOCIAL WORKER: Yes, I can understand you [GI].

CLIENT: It makes me mad when people can't understand me. I am trying to speak as clearly as I can.

SOCIAL WORKER: Thank you, no, I am not having a problem at all. Some of the things we could talk about are the things that you mentioned, as being independent, working with people, or we could talk about other things [GI—agenda setting].

CLIENT: I don't talk to other people much. I can get along, I know I need some help in some places, oh I don't know. I'm not sure about what to do. I like living on the streets. Nobody is my boss. I can do what I want. Every time I get into one of these housing things I can't help but getting into trouble. Other places have told me, "You're going to get into trouble. You have to stay on your medications." So I do that for awhile, and I do get better, but I hate dealing with other people. That's why I lost my job. This idiot at work, I was doing this gardening job, and he didn't understand me. And I was trying to speak clearly. You know, my medications gave me that stupid problem with my speech. That's the other thing, they told me that's from the medication. That's what scares me. I am already hard to understand. Then it makes me mad and I lose control and I know I should stop but I don't know what to do. I really get nervous. I get nervous about my meds.

SOCIAL WORKER: So even just thinking about this list of things that we have been talking about is kind of scary [CR].

CLIENT: Yeah, yeah.

SOCIAL WORKER: And yet you like being on your own, you like being your own boss, and there are also times it's not so great [CR—double-sided reflection].

CLIENT: I like living outside, I like it. But I got mugged, beat up.

SOCIAL WORKER: People take advantage of you. You have some ideas about being on your own, about being independent, and doing it in a way where you don't get taken advantage of. You also have some concerns about taking your medication and about getting along with people. People have been mean to you [SR—summary].

CLIENT: Everyone wants something from you. That's why I am not jumping in here. That's why I am taking my time here. It seems nice, but you know, you might have some other reason for me to be here. I'm not up for this.

SOCIAL WORKER: You are thinking that we might have some ideas that have nothing to do with what you want [CR].

CLIENT: Yeah, yeah. I've been down this road before. I'm not an idiot. I went to school. I know what's going on. I have reasons. I have had some bad experiences.

SOCIAL WORKER: You've learned to trust yourself and be careful with some people, be cautious with them. That's a way to protect yourself [MIA—affirming].

CLIENT: Is that bad to want to protect yourself?

SOCIAL WORKER: I don't think so [GI]; what do you think [OQ]?

CLIENT: I don't think so. I think that's the only way I am staying alive. I've slept under a bridge for a week. I know how to move, how to get around. I know where the cops are. I know where there are going to be people who cause me a problem, so I can live like that. I know what to do.

SOCIAL WORKER: You have some skills around caring for yourself, protecting yourself [MIA—affirming]. What kinds of skills do you have that help you, in working with a roommate [OQ]?

CLIENT: I've been at this a long time, I know the deal. If you don't go with the rules, they kick you out. I know that. Some guys I've lived with don't get that, they just kind of fight it. I figure, if I'm not going someplace, just do the deal. It's either do the deal, and stay in, or don't do the deal, and get kicked out and be on my own.

SOCIAL WORKER: You know how to follow the rules and get along, even when people around you aren't being real helpful [SR]. What else do you know how to do well [OQ]?

CLIENT: I like to garden. Even when I was a kid, I had a garden with vegetables. But my old man was a jerk. He would mess it up, criticize me, tell me I was a sissy. But he was a mean old man. They threw me out when I got in trouble, when I went in the hospital when I was 16. And I never went back. But I remember I really liked growing stuff. That's why I thought that job I had was cool, but the boss was a jerk. But I can make stuff grow.

SOCIAL WORKER: You are good at making stuff grow, being in a garden [SR].

CLIENT: And being outside ...

SOCIAL WORKER: You like being outside. You like that [SR].

CLIENT: I know, I know, the way I do well is when I am on my meds. But here's the thing I don't trust. I know I do better when I am on my medications. But they make my speech worse. The meds help me feel better but then I have to go back to the hospital all the time, they keep tracking me, it's a way for them to keep track of where I am. They don't like it that I'm homeless. They don't like it ... and I think, "Why don't you stay out of my business? I'm my own boss. I'm just laying low." But then I think, if I don't take my medication, then I go to that dark place where I get real low, real low, and I then I don't want to do anything. I know I can be better on my meds but I don't like all that checking, checking ...

SOCIAL WORKER: You feel two ways about it; on the one hand, it's all the checking and feeling like you have to be accountable to someone and the reporting in, and on the other hand, you know that the meds make you feel better and that they help you get along with people [CR].

CLIENT: Can't we just have meds without all that checking? Can't they just give them to me? I mean, I don't like them in my business all of the time. Maybe there's a new medication.

SOCIAL WORKER: You have done well on your medication in the past and you have jumped through all of the hoops that it takes, you were able to live with a roommate and get along, and you were able to work a job you liked for awhile [MIA—affirming].

CLIENT: I just don't know if I can do all of the other stuff. I get really overwhelmed. It just seems like too much for me, any kind of a job.

SOCIAL WORKER: What did you like about the job, besides being outside and gardening [OQ]?

CLIENT: Nobody messed with me. I didn't have to deal with the customers. I could just be out there, moving flats around, I felt like I was on my own.

SOCIAL WORKER: It's important for you to be independent [CR].

CLIENT: I always have been. I think I can do better. I always keep myself clean. That's why I came for a shower. Even when I am out on my own, it is important for me to look good. I know that people look at me. I like to be clean as much as I can. I get pretty creative about that. I can figure out a way to get water.

SOCIAL WORKER: So that's another skill you have, in terms of the way of taking care of yourself [MIA—affirming]. It's important for you to stay clean and be able to socialize with other people [SR].

CLIENT: You know, my sister is the only one in my family who has been really nice to me. My parents basically ditched me when I got sick. I probably gave them reason. I haven't been a good son. I stay away from them. But I do go over to my sister's house every once in awhile and she has kids, so I try to stay looking clean.

SOCIAL WORKER: That's important to you [SR].

CLIENT: Yeah.

SOCIAL WORKER: What do you like about being an uncle [OQ]?

CLIENT: Wow … I like that they just kind of come up and give me a hug, they haven't been "programmed" the way others have been been.

SOCIAL WORKER: They accept you for who you are [CR].

CLIENT: Yeah.

SOCIAL WORKER: And it helps that you are clean. And that you care for them, be social with them, and the medication helps you do that [SR].

CLIENT: I hadn't really thought of that. But that is the one place in my family where I feel connected. With my sister and her kids. And her husband is ok with me. She doesn't want me to live there, but she gives me meals sometimes.

SOCIAL WORKER: So she cares about you and helps you stay independent [SR].

CLIENT: My brother and my dad, they're jerks. They have a business together. They're toxic. I know they're plotting against me. They just haven't been able to get in and mess up my sister's mind. They're coming after me.

SOCIAL WORKER: But your sister you have found to be helpful and supportive [SR].

CLIENT: She won't me let come if I've been drinking. And that's hard, cause if I got the money, I want to drink.

SOCIAL WORKER: She doesn't want her kids to see you drinking [CR].

CLIENT: Yeah, so I, that's where I go.

SOCIAL WORKER: So when you want to see your sister and her kids, you stay sober [SR]. That's another skill you have, you are able to stay sober when you put your mind to it [MIA—affirming].

CLIENT: I hadn't thought about it as a skill, I feel like a bum.

SOCIAL WORKER: It sounds like you have a bunch of different skills: from what you told me: you like to work in the garden, you like to be outside, you know how to follow the rules, you know that you are bright ... [SR—summary].

CLIENT: I did good in school, before I got sick. But I think my parents are plotting against me. They didn't want me in the house. They want me to fail.

SOCIAL WORKER: In spite of all of this, you have been able to succeed at many things [MIA—affirming/support]: staying sober, getting along with a roommate, working, following rules around places, and getting your blood drawn when you don't want to [SR]. You do a lot of healthy things for yourself [MIA—affirming/support].

CLIENT: If I could live in the way I want, that's what I want, to be independent. If I have to take medication, I will, I just want to be able to come and go.

SOCIAL WORKER: You are willing to take meds because if you don't take them, you lose your freedom and when you do take them, you are able to be free and independent [CR—double-sided reflection]. Speaking of getting what you want, if it is OK with you [MIA—asking permission], I was wondering if we could take a look at this form [the CANSAS-P] that you filled out during your intake, about some of the services we provide. If we could look at this together, maybe you could tell me what your thinking was when you filled it out. Looking at it, you filled out that you needed some help with accommodations or a place to live, daytime activities, feeling sad or low, alcohol use, friends or company, money, benefits, and information about your medication [GI]. Which one of these, if any, would you like to discuss with me [OQ]?

CLIENT: I'm living outside. If I am to get into a place of my own, I'm going to need some help, I don't have any money. Who's going to trust me?

SOCIAL WORKER: One of the things you would like is not to have a roommate and to live in a place by yourself [SR].

CLIENT: If I have to have a roommate, I can do that, but I tend to get in trouble. If I'm on medication, then I'm easier to live with. But I would need help. Who would take me in?

SOCIAL WORKER: You are thinking then that you would be willing to go somewhere where others live instead of getting your own apartment [SR].

CLIENT: I can do that.

SOCIAL WORKER: You wrote on here that you already get help with food, meals [GI].

CLIENT: Yes, my sister helps me out, I go to food pantries. Even if they have strings some times. That guy who found me living in the bushes told me that this program would help me with housing, help me get hooked up with services, if I'm eligible.

SOCIAL WORKER: That is certainly something we can work on [GI]. What else on this list would you like to talk about [OQ]?

CLIENT: I'm bored all day now. It was OK when I had my job, I liked that. I liked being busy. I get in trouble when I'm not busy. That's when I start thinking I need a drink. I'm just sitting around, bored. When I had a roommate, before I got my job, then I hated that, just sitting around. When I worked, I came home tired and just wanted to go to sleep. If it weren't for that jerk of a boss, I would have been OK.

SOCIAL WORKER: So that's another skill you have [MIA—affirming], you like to stay busy and work hard. That's important for you. You would like some help with getting a job because this also keeps you from getting bored [SR].

CLIENT: Well, you know, I get real slow, especially if I am not on my medication. And I just don't want to do anything, so that's a problem. Most of the time I just don't want to meet anybody, I'm just stewing my life away. That's hard.

SOCIAL WORKER: It's more helpful for you, when you are on your medication, to be working and staying busy. The meds also help you talk to other people and be less lonely [SR].

CLIENT: I don't know much about my meds other than I don't like how they make me feel. I want to see about getting something different, where I don't have to be checked on either.

SOCIAL WORKER: It is important for you to find out about the side effects of you meds and maybe see if something else will work instead [SR].

CLIENT: I think so. I want to talk to the doctor. That's for sure.

SOCIAL WORKER: If it is OK with you, I would like to ask you about "psychological distress" [MIA—asking permission]. You put that it is a met need [GI].

CLIENT: Well I get lonely because of all that is going on, but I feel better talking to you. But I'm not thinking about doing anything to myself, no way! And I get mad at people but I have never hurt anyone. I can manage my temper. I've been through a million of these. I just want to live on my own. I am OK. I've been a lot worse than this.

SOCIAL WORKER: Coming here has helped a bit with connecting with other people, and this is something you might like to do more frequently, as long as you can live independently [CR].

CLIENT: That fight with my roommate … I know that when I got mad, everybody freaked out, they had to call in the troops. But they don't know how to deal with me. As I'm saying that, I know that I have to do better with my temper. That's one place I am not very good. If someone ticks me off, then I just want to knock 'em. But I can't do that. My sister told me that, you can't be like that.

SOCIAL WORKER: You are working on your temper [SR]. And there are times when you are able to control your temper [MIA—affirming].

CLIENT: You know, that job. I wasn't getting money but I liked it. If I could get a job where I got paid, I would really work on my temper.

SOCIAL WORKER: What else on this list would you like to go over with me [OQ]?

CLIENT: I like to drink, mainly when I'm bored, or lonely. Or it helps with my symptoms, like the voices. I know not everybody hears them and I get in trouble when I drink.

SOCIAL WORKER: And you are able to stay sober when you put your mind to it [MIA—support/affirming], like when you want to see your sister's kids [CR].

CLIENT: I need money to get a nice place. Maybe I can get a job that pays me. I'm not real good with money. That's maybe a skill I need. I would like some help about looking into what else I could get too.

[Discussion proceeds regarding items on the CANSAS-P.]

SOCIAL WORKER: To wrap up, Robert, you might be interested in working together regarding housing, your medication, getting a job, finances, and relationships [SR]. What have I missed [OQ]?

CLIENT: (*pause*) Can you help me see if there is any hope for me?

SOCIAL WORKER: You are concerned that as we sit here and talk about these things, things might not change, yet you would really like your life to be better [CR].

CLIENT: You got it. Everybody in my world says I'm worthless.

SOCIAL WORKER: They don't see the skills you have, that you know how to control your temper when you want to, that you know how to not drink, you can work hard, know how to take care of yourself, and how to be a good uncle to your sister's kids, but you know that and now I know that as well [MIA—affirming].

CLIENT: Most people have told me what's wrong with me. I know that stuff. Nobody has ever put it that way, telling me I have skills.

SOCIAL WORKER: I appreciate how open you have been with me [MIA—affirming]. The next time we meet, if it is alright with you, maybe we can start to prioritize this list. I want to hear your ideas of how we can work on these things together [GI].

CLIENT: OK, thanks.

DISCUSSION

In this interview, the social worker's goals were to engage Robert and begin to learn about his perspective on his life, including his concerns as well as the skills and relationships he has that could support him in his recovery. The direction of the interview was to motivate him to engage in treatment and to use his medication. Using the "MI assessment sandwich" approach, the social worker began the interview with simple reflections and she explained the purpose of the interview. Next she used agenda setting to also facilitate engagement, putting the decisions for the content of the discussion on Robert. She listed possible topics as a way to keep him organized. The social worker avoided reflecting more negatively charged statements that Robert made, for this would have taken the focus away from the goals of the interview as well as kept the tone of the interview as problem-oriented. Using self-affirmation theory, the social worker finds that the task is to have clients tell the interviewer about their areas of competence. Typical assessment interviews may ask for detailed information about prior hospitalizations, suicide attempts, active symptoms, and prescribed medications. This assessment interview was about the client as person; the social worker spent time in the initial part of the interview by exploring Robert's concerns as well as learning about the interests and skills he already has. She summarized frequently and provided many affirmations.

Some of the other MI skills that the social worker used were double-sided reflections, where she reflected Robert's ambivalence. In using this type of reflection, it is helpful to end with what we want the client to really remember and to use the word "and" to connect the statements. This helps underscore for clients that people can have both thoughts at the same time; it is not one way or another. The social worker elicited his feelings about being an uncle and connected the importance of maintaining these relationships with his medication adherence.

Later in the interview, the CANSAS-P was introduced, changing the flow of the free dialogue but still allowing for discussion of both unmet needs and areas where Robert was already doing well (i.e., self-care). These unmet needs were areas where Robert himself articulated that he needed help. Using a structured tool in this instance can also be helpful to keep clients on track (Carey et al., 2007). In the next meeting, the social worker might ask Robert to prioritize the list from the CANSAS-P and ask him for his ideas on how he might approach a particular need. As they work together to address the various needs, the social worker can also ask Robert, with permission, to share her feedback from her own list where she saw

Robert as needing some support (such as regarding psychological distress) and negotiate working on these areas as well.

FINAL THOUGHTS

Use of MI in an assessment interview provides us a way to engage with clients and set the stage to privilege their voices. They discuss their expertise on their lives and what is important to them. Information that may be needed or required by the agency most likely will arise freely in the course of the interview. Written assessment measures can also be integrated into the interview to provide another means to determine clients' expressed and felt needs. We can target specific core concerns after having a more global discussion about them with our clients. Curiosity that is used in an eliciting, listening, and affirmative manner may help us get to know our clients better than we would have imagined.

4

Supporting Self-Efficacy, or What If They Don't Think They Can Do It?

WITH STÉPHANIE WAHAB AND KATIE SLACK

When training MI, trainers often start out the day by asking train-ees, who are usually social workers and other helping professionals, what they already do in their work to motivate clients to change their behav-iors. Trainers know that trainees most likely use many of the skills of MI and want to elicit from their audience the knowledge and capabilities that exist as applied to their area of practice. Likewise, when using MI with individual clients, practitioners might ask what clients already know about a particular area, what similar kinds of changes they have made in the past, and/or what strengths or skills in general they already possess. Both trainees and clients answer these questions based on their particular contexts as this is where their expertise lies. We learned in Chapter 2 that self-affirmation theory (Sherman & Cohen, 2006; Steele, 1988) tells us that humans want to be seen as capable and if they either self-affirm or receive affirming information they are more open when addressing other areas that may be sensitive to discuss. Exploring what one knows about a particular topic or disclosing important positive values or characteristics can be used as a way to self-affirm, as well as a means to support client self-efficacy.

Self-efficacy is the belief that one is able to make a change or succeed in a specific task (Bandura, 1994, 1999). Self-efficacy theory holds that people's beliefs in themselves come from several sources. The most salient source is a successful achievement in a similar area. Thus, if I (MH) know that I have done fairly well in teaching and training MI over the past 10 years, then I should be able to do some writing about it, to convey concepts and ideas to readers. My self-efficacy regarding this book is pretty strong; now if this was a novel I was attempting, then it would be much lower! The second way that people gain self-efficacy is through observing someone similar to ourselves go through a certain experience or achieve something, also known as modeling. The thinking is, "If they can do it, I can do it." The third source, which is somewhat weaker, is through persuasion or someone else telling us that we can do it. A coach might convince a runner that he can go even faster. Of course, when he does, then his self-efficacy comes from having actually achieved the goal (back to our most salient source). The least effective source, according to Bandura (1994) is through the reduction of stress or negative mood state regarding the behavior or change. Someone who used to regard public speaking as something that would turn their stomach into a churning mess may no longer associate it with nausea and in fact will forget that it ever used to make them feel this way. This loss of a physiological response can come from practice and, again, from having achieved success in this area.

These two theories, self-affirmation theory and self-efficacy theory, can help us as we think about how to actually put into practice the MI principle of supporting self-efficacy. The use of affirmations in our practice with clients is one way to support self-efficacy, whereby we comment on client successes in similar areas and help them to make connections between past achievements/changes and the one under discussion. Acknowledging and supporting autonomy to make choices is another way to support self-efficacy. But some questions arise. What if our clients have never tried to change or practice the behavior under discussion or anything remotely similar to it? Or what if they have tried and failed? What if role models or other examples aren't available to them? Does persuasion really work? What if the psychosocial stressors our clients face are so numerous that gaining ground in any one area seems daunting and overwhelming, to both clients and social workers? Is it possible for clients to want to make changes but have absolutely no confidence in themselves to do it? What then? We will look at all of these concerns and apply MI to a client vignette where this occurs frequently: intimate partner violence.

AFFIRMATIONS REVISITED

Affirmations are statements that we make regarding clients' strengths, competencies, characteristics, or past successes. As Rosengren (2009) states, they "are a way of reorienting the client to the resources he or she has available for this effort … [they] communicate a prizing or appreciating clients for who they are " (p. 62). Rosengren recommends that affirmations begin with the word "you" to focus on clients' efforts or characteristics, but they should not be evaluative or judgmental. In other words, an affirmation would be something like, "You showed a lot of courage when you left your home country and family without knowing what was ahead."

When should we use affirmations? Probably a bit more frequently than we think. Using affirmations may also help us to keep from getting overwhelmed when we work with clients who have many areas of concern, as using affirmations keeps us focused on the positives and their strengths. They also may help us build rapport and respectfully engage with our clients as well as reduce possible resistance. Research using self-affirmation theory has indicated that study subjects were much more open to hearing negatively charged health-related information after they had participated in a self-affirming exercise on an entirely different topic (Reed & Aspinwall, 1998). People seem to become more open and less defensive when they have been affirmed (Sherman & Cohen, 2006).

Leffingwell and colleagues (2007) recommend using affirmations and positive discussions before problem areas are even explored as they have such a profound effect on clients. Using these findings, Carl Ake Farbring, a Swedish psychologist and MINT member, asks new clients at the start of interviews to describe who they are as people: their personal interests, what they are good at, things that they feel confident in, and/or what makes them happy (personal communication, June 27, 2010). Starting off an interview with a discussion of positive attributes or skills can increase willingness to be open or vulnerable in clients as they realize that their social worker doesn't just define who they are by their problems. Farbring, who works with prisoners, also stated, "Clients in my world are desperate to hear positive things about themselves because they seldom do."

SOURCES OF SELF-EFFICACY

As indicated above, Bandura (1994) found that self-efficacy can be increased through four processes: achievement in a similar area, modeling others, persuasion, and decreased negative mood states and responses. We will cover the first three processes as they most directly relate to MI.

Achievements in Similar Areas

Just as we saw in Chapter 3, using a strengths orientation, when we are interviewing clients we want to be vigilant to prior successes or characteristics that may be helpful to clients in the change process (Miller & Rollnick, 2002). We can affirm these strengths and also provide hope that further change is possible as clients have demonstrated that they have what they need to take steps to do things differently. Even prior failures at change efforts can be reframed as persistence (Rosengren, 2009). When we listen carefully, reflecting what clients are telling us about their story, we can return to these statements and begin to make connections: "Just as it took courage for you to leave your home country, your same courage will help you when you go on the job interview and face another new unknown."

Encouraging clients to think about small steps they might take in the change process may also provide them with achievements that will build self-efficacy. For instance, we, as social workers, might ask a client, "If you were to look for a job, what might you do first?" "What ideas do you have about how you might begin this process?" Discussing these first steps can also be done in an affirmative way: "What did you learn about yourself by going to get that job application?" Taking steps and then thinking about what was accomplished are ways for clients to observe themselves as capable.

Modeling or Observing Others

Sometimes clients can't imagine making the change(s) they are thinking about. If appropriate to the conversation, in MI we can offer information, with permission: "Would you be interested in hearing how some of my other clients went about living independently?" In this instance, it is helpful to give clients a *menu of options* to select from, that is, give clients several different examples (Rollnick et al., 2008) of what some of your other clients may have done: "Some have gone back to school to learn a specific job or trade; others have looked for work in a certain area; others have applied for state benefits to help them get on their feet." This also helps to support client autonomy, which in itself may increase self-efficacy, as we are treating our clients as capable adults who can make decisions about the right paths for themselves.

Persuasion or Providing Hope

Maybe you are scratching your head at this point and saying, "Persuasion? Isn't that a good way to increase resistance?" and you are probably right. Too often we try to persuade our clients (and friends and family members!) to do certain things only to have it backfire on us. So how do we take Bandura's finding that persuasion—his term—is a method, albeit weak, of increasing self-efficacy and apply it in an MI fashion? Perhaps one way is to reframe persuasion as encouragement. One of the areas that Miller and Rollnick (2002) emphasize in supporting self-efficacy is to supply hope to our clients. Projecting a hopeful, positive attitude may be an indirect way of persuading clients that change is possible. We aren't telling them to go ahead, do it, you'll do great and everything will be fine, but we can project this with our attitude. We know that others have accomplished certain tasks and, with some support, if needed, our clients can do it as well.

Through the use of reflective listening and specific questions, we can listen for and perhaps evoke *ability change talk* from clients. Ability change talk includes words and phrases such as able, can, I have, I did before, I know I can (Rosengren, 2009). As clients hear themselves speak, and we reflect or emphasize these words back to them, they indirectly persuade themselves that they have the skills or characteristics to make changes (self-perception theory). In a way, this is eliciting self-affirming statements. In thinking about change, it is important to differentiate between the *importance* of the change to clients and the *confidence* to make those changes. Some clients for instance may not think it is important to quit gambling; however, they may know that they have quit drinking successfully so that if they chose to quit gambling, they would know what to do. Other clients realize that they have endured the pain of intimate partner violence and want it to end, but they lack confidence in their abilities to make any changes in their relationships, for a variety of reasons that are discussed below. Confidence can rise or lower, like ambivalence, and we want to work toward both higher levels of importance and confidence (Miller & Rollnick, 1991).

Ability change talk may emerge naturally in an MI conversation, particularly as clients feel that they are being heard and respected without judgment. If change talk doesn't arise, one way to determine where clients stand regarding these two aspects of change is to use a *change ruler*, which is a series of scaling questions (Rollnick, Miller, & Butler, 2008). Clients are asked, "On a scale of 0–10, how confident are you that you can make this change?" "Why is it a __ and not a [lower number]?" "What would it take for you to, say, move up one number?" Reflections and summaries are used throughout this dialogue.

Clients will give us reasons why they may be a little bit confident, and they hear themselves a second time as we reflect the reasons back: "You have done this before and were successful for awhile and you know that when you put your mind to something, you stick to it. What else?" Obviously this takes us back to method #1 where clients are persuading themselves that they do have the capabilities and characteristics to get things done in their lives. We aren't persuading them; we are only evoking their thoughts and perspectives from them. Asking clients what would make them even more confident is a way of beginning to plan the small steps that they think they might take.

WHEN CONFIDENCE IS VERY LOW

An example of social work practice where we might find clients who are low in their self-efficacy is in intimate partner violence (IPV). Clients who are survivors of IPV often experience a compromised sense of self-confidence or self-efficacy when considering change in certain aspects of their lives. Emotional and psychological abuse coupled with isolation—all common elements of IPV—can lead survivors to doubt themselves and their abilities, as well as experience hesitancy or fear in making autonomous decisions. It can be a real challenge to empower and support self-efficacy in clients who have had those qualities literally and metaphorically beaten out of them through various forms of violence and abuse. We use MI to collaboratively engage clients, tap into their expertise and wisdom, suspend judgment, and honor autonomy. All of these skills and the MI spirit can be effective in enhancing clients'/survivors' self-efficacy and confidence, as limited as it may be. Survivors report the impact of being listened to as helpful and healing (Goodman & Epstein, 2008; McLeod, Hays, & Chang, 2010).

Because MI is simultaneously client-centered and directive, clients are supported to choose the behaviors they wish to explore and possibly address while we work with them in the direction of change. However, survivors should never be coerced or pushed to change something they are not ready or willing to change. Once again, in this area of practice especially, we work to resist the *righting reflex*—the desire to make better, fix, or prevent harm (Miller & Rollnick, 2002)—before clients have specifically asked for such assistance or given permission to provide it. When working in the area of IPV, the urgency and pull to protect and persuade survivors to make changes can be heightened, particularly when their life and relationship circumstances are deemed life-threatening by a provider (Motivational Interviewing and Intimate Partner Violence Work Group, 2010).

Privileging leaving (Wahab, 2006) refers to the systematic practice of prioritizing leaving the abuser (by practitioners and researchers alike) above all other possible options for change. If we impose leaving as the desired behavior/outcome, we can inadvertently replicate the same controlling behaviors that survivors experience with their abusive partners. This is not to argue that battered individuals should not leave their abusive partners; however, service providers must recognize that individuals may not always prioritize, for numerous reasons, leaving the abusive relationships. And even when they do prioritize leaving, clients may not be ready, or they may lack the motivation and confidence necessary to leave. Individuals from marginalized and oppressed communities including low-income, immigrant, refugee, disabled, and communities of color do not always have resources or access to resources necessary to leave, and ultimately live independently from their abusive partners (Wahab, 2006).

Such desire to protect an IPV survivor can have a paradoxical effect in that the more we argue the case for change, the natural response is for clients to provide the other side of the argument (reactance theory) and to possibly disengage from services (Grauwiler, 2008; Miller & Rollnick, 2002). This may in turn *lower* self-efficacy as clients may not feel understood and think that their situation is hopeless. Wahab (2006) suggests that when considering the use of MI with survivors involved in violent relationships, it is vital to keep in mind that IPV occurs within the context of a relationship. Individuals in abusive relationships have control only over their own behaviors; they cannot control the behaviors of their partners, nor should they be encouraged to do so. Despite taking action and changing one's behaviors, a violence-free life cannot always be secured. Consequently, it is important to keep in mind that if we are going to use MI in IPV or other similar contexts, it is vital to focus on the target behaviors that clients can control and want to change, especially when we wish to support and increase self-efficacy around any kind of change.

While not a homogeneous population, IPV survivors frequently choose to address within an IPV service setting concerns that include, but are not limited to (1) safety planning (i.e., restraining orders, safety plans, harm reduction, self-care, or leaving the relationship); (2) substance use (drugs, alcohol, food, medication); (3) parenting; (4) health and mental health issues; (5) compliance with program rules; (6) self-care; and/or (7) employment or housing (Nurius & Macy, 2010). The following client vignette demonstrates MI methods to support self-efficacy: reflective listening, affirmations, providing options, and responding to and eliciting ability change talk.

IPV: EXAMPLE AND DIALOGUE

Najuah is a 35-year-old survivor of IPV. She is a mother of three girls, ages 4, 8, and 10, and has been married to their father for 12 years. The family members are all legal residents and hold green cards. Najuah's husband has always been a bit controlling and jealous; he became more violent once Najuah became pregnant with their second child. Najuah has experienced multiple forms of violence from her husband over the course of the past 10 years. The violence has intensified over the years, and her husband's latest violent outburst put her in the hospital for two days. Najuah does not have any immediate family in the United States. All of her close family lives in the Middle East. Najuah and her family are practicing Muslims and are very involved with their Mosque and its community. The family identifies as middle class. Her husband works full time as an engineer, and Najuah is not currently working outside of the home. While in the hospital, a social worker referred her to a nonprofit social service agency that provides multiple forms of support and advocacy to immigrants, including IPV counseling. A report was made to Child Protective Services (CPS) and the father has agreed to leave the home, while the case is under investigation. Najuah is being seen on an outpatient basis at a women's counseling center and is meeting with her counselor who is an MSW (at the agency) for the second time.

Once again, we will code the interactions using the following:

* GI = giving information
* SR = simple reflection
* CR = complex reflection
* OQ = open-ended question
* CQ = closed-ended question

* MIA = MI adherent (affirming, asking permission, emphasizing personal control, support)

SOCIAL WORKER: Hi Najuah, thank you for coming in today. How have things been since we met last week [OQ]?

CLIENT: OK, well, not very good. The woman who came to our house, the [CPS] social worker, said that it would be better if my husband were to move out now. I don't understand, he's a good man, he gives us everything we need, and he loves the children. Why should he have to leave?

SOCIAL WORKER: It sounds like a lot has been happening and that you feel overwhelmed and confused by what the social worker is asking of you and your family [CR].

CLIENT: Yes, how is it their place to tell us what to do? Like I said, he is a good man. He didn't mean to hurt me and he would never hurt our children. He takes good care of them. It was all a big mistake and really was my fault.

SOCIAL WORKER: Your husband provides for you and your children and he loves them very much [SR; avoids the "expert trap" (becoming the expert instead of the collaborator) by not explaining the role of CPS or educating about abuse].

CLIENT: He does, I know there have been times that he was feeling stressed and he was not being himself, but he loves them very much. And how would I take care of the children on my own if he were to stay away permanently?

SOCIAL WORKER: So on the one hand you know he loves you and the children, and on the other hand you see sometimes that he is not himself with them or you [CR].

CLIENT: Well, yes, he has raised his voice before and sometimes I'm scared they will do something to upset him or that I will say the wrong thing. And now they say he should move out. (*Starts to cry.*) I don't know what to do.

SOCIAL WORKER: And you are really doing everything you can to try to figure that out and care for all your family [MIA—support].

CLIENT: Yes (*tearful*). But I don't think I can manage a family by myself. This is just too much for me to do.

SOCIAL WORKER: Najuah, you love your family so much and you are focused on taking care of them [MIA—affirming]. I'm wondering about other challenges you've faced in your life, tell me about a time in the past when you faced something really hard [OQ; asking for past successes]?

CLIENT: When I left my home country, that was very difficult; I didn't know what would happen to me when I left or to my family that stayed behind. I was so worried.

SOCIAL WORKER: What helped you then [OQ]?

CLIENT: I prayed, my faith. I have my friends who are also from my country. Also there's a lady, a neighbor, and she has always been very kind to me—ever since we first moved here, and sometimes we'll sit and have tea and she'll talk to me, she always makes me feel better. (*Straightens up and stops crying.*)

SOCIAL WORKER: Your faith and spending time with friends and your neighbor are both things that you discovered really helped you when times were hard [MIA—support].

CLIENT: Yes, and I pray now, all the time, when I'm trying to figure out what to do. It helps. But I am too embarrassed to tell my friends what happened.

SOCIAL WORKER: So much has been happening in your life, and you are working very hard trying to figure out what to do [MIA]. If it is OK with you, I wonder if we could take a step back now, and look at this list—there are a few different ways that we could spend our time together today and it really is up to you to decide what you think would be most helpful [MIA]. Does that sound OK [CQ]?

SOCIAL WORKER: (*Shows Najuah a list comprised of various areas for the focus of the counseling—including safety, self-care/stress management, parenting, healthy relationships, social support, job searching, and problem solving—and explains each one briefly.*) Which one of these, if any, would you like to spend some time talking about today [CQ]?

CLIENT: OK, I think job searching maybe. If he does have to move out for a while, I might need to get part-time work at least. I did work at a store at home; I even helped with the books. I'm good with money.

SOCIAL WORKER: So you know one skill you have is working with money and you have experience in that area too [SR].

CLIENT: Yes, I helped in my family's store back home sometimes. Actually, my other neighbor, her husband has a market in our neighborhood, maybe they would let me work at their store.

SOCIAL WORKER: You want to talk to your neighbor and see if working in their store might be an option [SR].

CLIENT: I could. At least if I could do a small amount of work, maybe my husband wouldn't even have to know about it ... I don't know how I would explain it to my friends if they were to see me. They might think badly of my husband that I have to work. Maybe I shouldn't do it; it wouldn't be enough money for all this bother.

SOCIAL WORKER: While you are worried about what your friends might think, you also thought some about maybe needing to find work because you would feel better if you knew you could bring some money in, especially if your husband has to move out for a while [CR]. You know that you're good with money, and you'd like to find out if your neighbor might be able to offer you work in his store [SR].

CLIENT: Yes, that might help. I could ask him. Who knows, maybe it would lead to a better job, though who would hire me, with my accent? What has happened with some of your other clients like me? What do they do?

SOCIAL WORKER: I have worked with many women who have not worked much since they were raising children. Some decide to go back to school for awhile before they get work, others work with a vocational counselor from the county to figure out what they want to do, and others have ideas and some connections much like you are describing [GI].

SOCIAL WORKER: As you think about inquiring about a job, how important is it for you to ask about this job, on a scale of 0 to 10, with 0 being "not important at all" and 10 being "extremely important" [OQ]?

CLIENT: An 8, I guess. I want to know that I could take care of what the children need if I had to.

SOCIAL WORKER: It feels pretty important to you to at least check into the possibility of working at your neighbor's store [SR].

CLIENT: Yes, they are very nice and the wife is always asking about the children, maybe I could work for them.

SOCIAL WORKER: What makes it so important for you to do this? Why are you an 8 and not, say, a 5 [OQ]?

CLIENT: I don't want to do this, but I know I might need to start making some money. Even if my husband comes back home, I want to contribute something. I have thought about this before. I just don't want him to think I am questioning him as a provider by going out to work. He gets so jealous.

SOCIAL WORKER: So even though it may make your husband upset, working is something you have thought about before [CR]. How confident are you that you could talk to your neighbors about this job should you decide to do so, on that same scale of 0 to 10 [OQ]?

CLIENT: Hmm, to talk to him, I guess maybe a 6 or 7, I feel nervous to ask them about it.

SOCIAL WORKER: You feel kind of nervous to talk to them and you have some confidence [SR]. What makes you somewhat confident at a 6 or 7 instead of say, a 4 or a 5 [OQ]?

CLIENT: Well, I know this family and I think they like me. I have worked doing this kind of thing before. I just don't know if they need help. What if they say no? What will I do then?

SOCIAL WORKER: It's hard when you don't know what the outcome will be [MIA]. What do you think might help you feel more confident that you could talk to them and move you up the scale, like to an 8 [OQ]?

CLIENT: I see the social worker this week; she said it would help if he would move out for awhile, and I know she is going to ask him about that. Hopefully, he won't have to move out for a long time, but that would make me want to do something, to try to find work.

SOCIAL WORKER: You would feel more confident and determined to find some work if he does decide he needs to move out [CR].

CLIENT: Yes, I would do it then, I would have to. It will be really difficult for us to afford the apartment we have and then get another one for him. He won't move in with friends as he doesn't want anyone to know our business.

SOCIAL WORKER: Let me make sure I've understood all that you've shared with me. A lot has happened in your life over the past few weeks. You are worried about what will happen if/when your husband moves out, at least for a period of time. You don't understand why the [CPS] social worker is suggesting he do this, you feel like he is a good man and loves the children and takes care of the family, at the same time you have seen him get stressed and not be himself with the girls, and sometimes you worry that he will get upset. You have thought about needing to find some work because you want to make sure your children have what they need. You know you are good with money, and you thought of the possibility of working for your neighbors and asking them if they have a job for you. You are nervous about asking them and feel like if your husband does indeed move out, you will certainly ask them about a job [SR]. Have I missed anything [CQ]?

CLIENT: No, that is it.

SOCIAL WORKER: I'm wondering, if it would be OK with you, if we could spend the next few minutes checking in about your safety, much like we talked about last week [MIA]. Would that be OK with you if ... [MIA—asking permission].

DISCUSSION

Supporting self-efficacy is critical for many of our clients, not just those who are IPV survivors. For instance, in the previous chapter, our client with serious mental illness asked his social worker toward the end of the interview if he was hopeless. In this chapter's vignette, the client, Najuah, vacillated back and forth between wanting to make changes in her life and being uncertain that she can do so. She offered change talk to her social worker and immediately countered it with sustain talk, or reasons why she couldn't get a job or move forward with her life. Her self-efficacy was low, and the social worker didn't argue with her or try to convince her that she has what it takes to make changes. The social worker also did not detract from the purpose of the session—to help the client resolve her ambivalence and move towards healthy change—by asking closed-ended questions aimed at eliciting the facts. For example, she could have asked: "What is the timeline the CPS worker gave you in terms of when your husband needs to move out?" These questions may become relevant later, in the action-planning stage, but could effectively impede progress at this point. Instead, the social worker stayed focused and used strategic questions to evoke from Najuah her own thoughts on her strengths and abilities. The social worker also strategically reflected her positive change talk but did not totally ignore her concerns.

The social worker supported Najuah's autonomy by not trying to convince Najuah that her relationship is violent and that she would be better off without her husband. Only Najuah can make this decision, particularly within the context of her own values and culture. The social worker also communicated respect by taking the time to reflect the client's statements (reflections) and highlight the client's strengths (affirmations) throughout the interview/session, the simplicity of which should not be devalued. IPV survivors may have few opportunities in their daily lives to feel listened to and respected. This seemingly basic level of acknowledgment can serve as a stepping stone to greater self-esteem and therefore in turn support the client's self-efficacy.

As the session progressed, Najuah chose to focus on job searching and truly only she can decide if even getting a job is the best option for her right now. Rollnick et al. (2009) term the stance that the social worker may take as "equipoise," which results when the social worker has no particular aspiration as to which direction the client should take. The social worker's task was to help Najuah sort through her options and assist her with planning. Most IPV social workers do have aspirations that clients will eventually remove themselves from violent relationships; however, when working in this area, we have to be careful to not let these aspirations influence us, as this decision is still ultimately up to the client (Motivational Interviewing and Intimate Partner Violence Workgroup, 2010). In addition, if we focus on only one side of the issue—the benefits of the client leaving the relationship—we fall into the trap of the righting reflex, as was previously mentioned, and risk eliciting further resistance from the client.

Clients such as Najuah can be overwhelming to social workers. This is often the case when we have clients with numerous important and competing issues that must be addressed and when they themselves are completely overwhelmed and stymied as to how to move forward. Sometimes clients just want their social workers to tell them what to do. In this vignette, the social worker used agenda setting to guide Najuah into an area that she wished to talk about. The social worker used a list of options that helped to parcel out various areas and give Najuah a sense of control of how she wanted to focus her time with her therapist. When asked, the social worker also provided her with a menu of options of how other clients have handled employment needs, again supporting her autonomy and wisdom in knowing what is best for herself. Allowing Najuah to prioritize the areas of change discussed in the session also served to lessen the degree to which she felt overwhelmed, and to help break the change process down into manageable parts. In this way, MI may offer clients an effective approach to problem solving in the future. In using the Readiness Ruler, Najuah indicated that her goal of talking to her neighbor about a job was very important to her and she was a little less confident in her ability to do this. When asked what would make her even more confident, she indicated that the urgency of the situation would force her to make a decision about asking for a job.

FINAL THOUGHTS

Many of the people we work with have challenges associated with self-efficacy or their beliefs in their abilities to change. Their ambivalence and low confidence to make changes causes them to waiver between wanting to make changes and having us, as their social workers, tell them what to do. When we ask clients to describe to us past positive experiences and/ or personal strengths, they are "persuading" themselves that perhaps they have what it takes. Reflecting these strengths back to them, and then summarizing them again, helps them hear themselves talk as well as gather a different perspective on themselves. Finally, it is important to remember that although getting a part-time job may not appear to be the most critical factor in an IPV situation, this one "small" change could lead to many other changes. The MI principle of supporting self-efficacy offers social workers an empowering focus much like has been emphasized in the battered women's movement (McDermott & Garofalo, 2004; Wahab, 2005b). Our hope is that our work with IPV clients will ultimately empower them to decide the terms of their lives and that these terms will not include abuse or violence of any kind.

5

Expressing Empathy
Communicating Understanding
(Even When It's Hard)

MI was started, as we learned in Chapter 2, when Bill Miller, as an intern, began to work with patients in alcoholism treatment and didn't know exactly what he was supposed to do. Being a student of Carl Rogers, he did know how to use reflective listening skills in a client-centered manner, which was not typical of alcohol treatment at that time. Miller found that his patients responded well and went on to be very open in their discussion of their problems and concerns. His research studies confirmed his experiential finding: the alcohol treatment clients who reduced their drinking had therapists who interacted with higher levels of empathy (Moyers, 2004).

Over the past half-century, Carl Rogers's work (1957) has continued to influence therapists and social workers, with his emphasis on the "core conditions" of empathy, unconditional positive regard (sometimes called acceptance), and congruence (sometimes known as genuineness). Practitioners are drawn to this humanistic approach, and decade after decade of research has continued to support the impact of Rogers's theory/model (Kirschenbaum & Jourdan, 2005) and the importance of empathy. A large study of the effect of the therapeutic relationship between the counselor or social worker and client found that the main ingredients of empathy, therapeutic alliance, and goal agreement had the strongest impacts on the client/practitioner relationship. The relationship was important for successful outcome, independent of the specific type of therapy used (Norcross, 2001). Based on this finding, it is easy to understand why one of the core principles of MI is to "express empathy" (Miller & Rollnick, 2002).

DEFINING EMPATHY

What do we mean by empathy? One of the best sources for a definition is Rogers's own version. He stated that empathy is "to perceive the internal frame of reference of another with accuracy, and with the emotional components and meanings which pertain thereto, as if one were the other person, but without ever losing the 'as if' condition ... [it is] to sense the hurt or the pleasure of another as he senses it, and to perceive the causes thereof as he perceives them, but without ever losing the recognition that is as if I were hurt or pleased, etc." (Rogers, 1959, pp. 210–211). Thus empathy involves understanding the world or problem as the client sees it without identifying with or taking on the problem.

Empathy is to be distinguished from sympathy, which is the expression of concern or compassion for another's problem or distress (Clark, 2010b). Expressions of sympathy can include, "I am so sorry that this happened to you" or "You poor thing, the world just seems to be falling apart for you." Sometimes when we teach or train MI, trainees confuse the two concepts and think that by entering the world of another and listening to it, that this somehow conveys acceptance or soft-heartedness. As one trainee, who was a probation officer, told a colleague, "I only have empathy for the victim!" Empathy is understanding the concern or problem from clients' perspectives. We can accept our clients as humans, and being empathic with them does not mean we accept or approve of certain behaviors (Miller & Rollnick, 2002).

Other definitions of empathy describe the relational or interactive aspect in the expression empathy. Empathy is

the practitioner's accurate perception of the internal frame of reference of a client and communicating this understanding to the person. (Clark, 2010a, p. 348)

the skillful and deliberate ability to convey a sense of being present, understanding the client's words, emotions, and underlying meaning. (Feldstein & Forcehimes, 2007, p. 738) the inhaling of another person's life experience, processing it through your own life experience, and exhaling a personal response that communicates that you are seeing, hearing, accepting, and understanding what the other person has been and is experiencing. (V. Keller, personal communication, September 2010)

These definitions address how empathy involves not only understanding what our clients are communicating but conveying this understanding back to them. Barrett-Lennard (1981, p. 94) calls this the "empathy cycle." As shown in Figure 5.1, in this cycle, clients express their thoughts, ideas, or feelings (Step 1). As social workers, we listen and attempt to understand the messages that clients are trying to convey, whether directly spoken or unspoken (Step 2, "empathic resonation"). We then express empathy by communicating statements that indicate an awareness of what our clients are experiencing or thinking (Step 3, "expressed empathy"). Clients then "receive" our empathy and (hopefully) feel a sense of being understood and listened to (Step 4, "received empathy"), which causes them to continue to communicate (Step 5, "fresh expression and resonation"), which is really

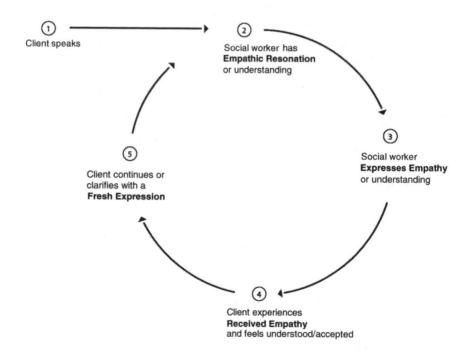

FIGURE 5.1. The empathy cycle (Barrett-Lennard, 1981).

Step 1 all over again. Expressing empathy encourages clients to continue to describe their concerns or thoughts. We learn what clients' perspectives are and in the process, they hear themselves think out loud, sometimes hearing their own internal arguments for the first time. Being listened to in a focused, nonjudgmental, accepting manner can be a new experience for some and allows clients to feel valued as individuals and be more open to discussion of uncomfortable topics (Myers, 2000; Rogers, 1957).

EMPATHY AS A PROCESS

Step 1: The Client Speaks

Using the empathy cycle (Barrett-Lennard, 1981) helps us to examine the process of expressing empathy. If expression of empathy is done in a relational context, what are the necessary ingredients? As we have discussed in earlier chapters, the spirit of MI provides the approach to our work with clients. If we convey respect, curiosity, and interest, with a focus on listening, we can set the groundwork for start of the empathy cycle. When we were social work students, we all learned about "attending skills" in our social work practice classes and became familiar with concepts of body language, appropriate eye contact, open posture, and so on (Hepworth, Rooney, Rooney, & Strom-Gottfried, 2010). These are the main skills that are needed in Step 1, where the client speaks. We create an atmosphere where clients are receiving all of our attention and feel our full focus. This can be especially difficult in interviewing clients in certain social work contexts, such as in clients' homes with TVs blasting or phones ringing (Kirst-Ashman & Hull, 2009). Interviewing clients in prisons, residential treatment centers, or shared offices can also be distracting. Social workers are good at working past these distractions. As clients feel our full focus, they become more likely to communicate more personal or important messages (Moyers, Miller, & Hendrickson, 2005). Using small talk and then a general open-ended question are good ways to invite clients to speak.

Step 2: Empathic Resonation

When clients speak, they may provide us messages that are quite direct; or their messages may be vague or unclear, or they may not necessarily express what they mean (Miller & Rollnick, 2002). So after clients speak, we work to figure out what exactly they are trying to tell us. We aim to understand their perspective and may need to take a guess as to what the real message is. All of this is filtered through our knowledge and experience, yet we strive to put aside our own values, reactions, and expectations.

A young undergraduate social work student reported that on her first day at her internship at a substance use treatment program, a client approached her and asked if she was in recovery. When she said no, that client then stated, "I don't listen to anyone who isn't in recovery!" The intern's gut reaction was to defend herself, and she launched into an explanation of her background, education, and the like. She knew she didn't handle this the way she wanted. As we reviewed the client's statement, using an MI perspective, I asked her what, if anything, she knew about this particular client or the clientele served by the agency. She knew that most of them were either homeless or had come to the program from prison; most had experienced some sort of physical or sexual abuse and related trauma; most had severe and chronic histories of drug addiction. In terms of meeting strangers, particularly those who are young, middle class, and well educated, it would seem that at least being in drug recovery would provide a common ground. Not trusting strangers can be a healthy coping skill that is learned in prison or on the streets. As we discussed these areas, the student began to experience empathic resonation: she put herself in her client's shoes. Given the context of the client's statement, it began to make sense. It is the client's view of the world and her experiences that frame the interactions. In using MI, we want to understand this worldview, not endeavor to have the client understand us and our reactions.

Step 3: Expressed Empathy

The main skill that is the foundation to expressing empathy is reflective listening, and Miller and Rollnick describe this as the most "challenging" of MI skills (2002, p. 67). We can repeat or rephrase what the client said, providing *simple reflections*. Sometimes these are useful in the early phases of a conversation, to simply encourage clients to keep talking and have them expand on their "story" or viewpoint. Typically reflections start with the word "you" (Miller & Rollnick, 2002), and as MI practitioners get more experience, sometimes even the "you" is dropped. Reflections are always statements, not questions. Questions can put clients on the spot and tend to be conversation "roadblocks" (Rosengren, 2009). A rephrase of the statement made by the client above might be, "You listen only to those who have experienced recovery."

As we interact with clients, in MI we want to strive for more in-depth reflections that go beyond what the client said or provide a deeper meaning. These are called *complex reflections*. We may have to make a guess as to what clients are trying to tell us, we may reflect the emotion beneath the statement, or we can "continue the paragraph" (Miller & Rollnick, 2002, p. 70) by anticipating and stating what we think clients might say next. Typically, if we are closely following what clients are saying, we won't be too far off base. And if we are, then clients will correct us and keep talking. It helps to think of a complex reflection as something of a hypothesis test when we are moving beyond something that the client has stated. We can also use *double-sided reflections* that help pull together for clients the ambivalence they feel: "You learned in prison not to talk to anyone and you know that working with counselors here will probably help you in your recovery." *Summaries* are typically long reflections that can "gather together" clients' various statements (Miller & Rollnick, 2002). Summaries let clients know that we have really listened and paid attention, and they help clients organize their thoughts.

Students and trainees who are learning MI sometimes worry that hypothesis testing is putting words in clients' mouths. They ask if would be better to "cushion" their reflection by introducing them with words such as "What I hear you saying is … ", or "It seems to me that … ", or "From what I can observe, it sounds like … " as it allows the social worker to be wrong and for the client to correct him or her. It feels uncomfortable for some to utilize reflections without this "cushioning," especially when they are trying to practice complex reflections. MI trainers encourage trainees to take a risk using "you … " statements and to see what happens (Rosengren, 2009). Taking the "I" out of a reflection keeps the focus on the client, allowing for empathic resonation, and clearer expression of empathy.

While all the types of reflections encourage clients to keep talking and to engage in the empathy cycle with us, the value of complex reflections over simple ones is that they help move the conversation forward (Tollison et al., 2008). Studies have found that using MI-consistent behaviors increases clients' willingness to engage with the therapist, be cooperative, and disclose more information (Catley et al., 2006; Miller, Benefield, & Tonigan, 1993; Moyers et al., 2005) and that MI-inconsistent behaviors, such as advising, directing, or warning, are related to clients' arguing or not being engaged (Apodaca & Longabaugh, 2009; Miller et al., 1993). Therapist use of reflective listening and other MI skills have also been found to be predictive of clients using change talk, which is turn is related to positive outcomes (Amrhein et al., 2003; Moyers et al., 2007).

What is also difficult in reflective listening is choosing what to reflect from all the statements our clients make and in deciding what kind of reflection (simple, complex, double-sided, a summary, etc.) would be most strategic. This is the directive aspect of MI, and we particularly want to listen for *client change talk* in the direction of where we are heading. In the above example, the initial goal of the social work intern would be to reduce the client's resistance and to begin to engage her in a therapeutic alliance. Once the client is engaged, the intern could utilize a guiding discussion about the goals the client has in mind for their work together. This helps provide the direction to move in. How and what to reflect comes with experience as well as feedback from the client, which leads us to the next step.

Step 4: Received Empathy

We can all think of a time when we discussed an important issue with a friend or family member and they really "got" what we were trying to say. They probably inadvertently used a reflective statement. It felt good to be understood, and it probably encouraged most of us to elaborate on the topic. One of the metaphors used in discussing the spirit of MI is the question of whether we are wrestling with our clients or if we are dancing. When trainees in an MI workshop hear this, they all nod their heads in understanding. Most of us know when we are doing one of these two things with our clients. Received empathy produces the dance. The dance is knowing that a connection has been made and that our "partner" is moving in sync with us. Self-determination theory tells us that humans have a need for relationships. Empathy via reflective listening helps us dance fairly quickly even with the most challenging of clients as they have felt heard and experience some sort of human connection.

Step 5: Fresh Expression

As clients feel connected, they are more likely to keep talking about their concerns (Catley et al., 2006; Miller et al., 1993). Being listened to without judgment or advice reduces resistance and allows clients to think about the possibility of change. In Step 5, clients continue the conversation, and the cycle continues as we utilize reflective listening statements, particularly complex reflections.

BUT IT CAN BE SO HARD AT TIMES ...

It is easy to jump out of the empathy cycle, for at least two reasons. One is that the "default" method of communication is to rely on questions, and when we fire off question after question, we fall into the question–answer trap. Miller and Rollnick (2002) call questioning the most "basic" of skills, and questions are certainly easy enough to ask. Questions also can keep us in control of the conversation, and they keep us on the hunt for information. Social workers are often in roles where they have to collect certain kinds of information.

While reflections are difficult, using them helps to make the interaction more of a collaborative partnership. Clients typically provide even more information in response to a good reflection than they would have to a specific question. If the relationship/engagement connection is made, clients will often tell us what we need to know without our ever having to ask a question.

The other reason that we leave the empathy cycle is that at times it can be very difficult to listen to someone describe behaviors or ideas that are out of sync with our value system or even legal society. Responding reflectively to statements regarding why it is OK to use drugs, be in a gang, not talk to a social worker, beat a wife, neglect children, cause a fight, can make us feel uncomfortable. This is especially true for social workers who are in some sort of social control position, such as those in CPS work or in criminal justice settings. One version of the righting reflex (the desire to fix or correct a problem) (Miller & Rollnick, 2002) kicks in when we want to challenge these kinds of statements, or educate, warn, advise, or even threaten clients. Our fear is that if we don't "correct" them, then we won't be doing our job. Or there is the worry that clients will think we are agreeing with them. MI practitioners struggle with this problem and work to *resist the righting reflex*. Some have found that a few cognitive strategies, such as reminding oneself that advice and threats typically do not change behavior, and that empathy does not equal agreement, can help.

Another method to resist the righting reflex is to utilize what Miller and Rollnick (2002) term as *coming alongside*. In MI, we recognize that most clients experience ambivalent feelings when thinking about making a change. When we come alongside of our clients, we reflect the more negative aspect of the change under discussion, also known as *sustain talk*. We do so to further the discussion and reduce resistance (Rosengren, 2009). An example might be, "Being in a gang gives you a place to belong." For practitioners who struggle with feeling that they are agreeing with the client's negative statements, reframing this as a resistance-reducing method called "coming alongside" helps with this worry. Rolling with resistance and knowing when to listen for and reflect sustain talk will also be explored further in Chapter 7.

Sometimes in MI we want to provide clients with information or share our thoughts with them. Although we work to evoke from clients what they already know, there may be times that clients need information they don't have. In this instance, MI practitioners use *elicit–provide–elicit* (EPE; Rollnick et al., 2008; Rosengren, 2009). First we elicit from clients what they already know regarding a certain topic. Then we provide the information or feedback, and then elicit again from clients what they think or we ask for their view. All of this is done in a respectful manner, to honor what clients already know and to make sure we support their autonomy. We can also offer a concern, as Rosengren (2009) states, when there is no clear way to broach the subject otherwise. Like EPE, we ask for clients' permission to offer a concern or thought, we provide it, and then we ask for their thoughts. This is all in keeping with the spirit of MI.

MI IN CPS WORK

One area where it can be a challenge to express empathy is working with parents who neglect their children, particularly those who are putting their own needs above those of their children. It is a cross-cultural value as well as a legal expectation that parents take care of their children. Children are vulnerable, and to have an adult willfully neglect or abuse them is difficult to see—and to hear.

Medical neglect is one of the smaller types of abuse to come to the attention of authorities, comprising about 2.3% of all substantiated cases of child maltreatment (U.S. Department of Health and Human Services, 2005), but it can be very serious. Medical neglect occurs when there is a parental "failure to heed obvious signs of serious illness or failure to follow a physician's instructions once medical advice has been sought" (Jenny et al., 2007, p. 1385). It has been found to be linked to other types of neglect, poor child growth and development, and even fatality (Dubowitz, 1999; Dubowitz et al., 2005). Children who are at risk for having serious medical problems due to parents not providing adequate care are usually reported to CPS by school personnel, social workers, or physicians. Lack of adequate or appropriate medical care can be caused by lack of access to medical services, poverty, family dysfunction, a religious reason, or parents' own lack of knowledge and skills (Jenny et al., 2007). Having a child with a chronic, serious illness can be stressful for any family, and this stress becomes multiplied when the family is concurrently facing other challenges (Dubowitz, 2011).

MI has only been studied in a few areas in CPS. The research is mainly limited to MI used to engage CPS parents in substance use treatment or in a parenting therapy (parent–child interaction therapy; see Carroll et al., 2001; Chaffin et al., 2009; Mullins, Suarez, Ondersma, & Page, 2004). Because parents are usually upset or resistant to the felt intrusion in their lives by the agency (Forrester et al., 2007), using MI can be helpful when the task is to engage parents in a working relationship with their social worker as well as to utilize treatment services (Hohman & Salsbury, 2009). One aspect of MI is to express empathy for what the parents are experiencing and the requirements being placed on them.

MEDICAL NEGLECT: EXAMPLE AND DIALOGUE

Denise is a 29-year-old white, married female who is the mother of two children, Paul, age 7 and Camden, age 5. Her husband has been deployed to Afghanistan for the past 8 months and the family lives in off-base housing. Camden was diagnosed with Type 1 diabetes when he was about 4 years old. Camden started kindergarten this year, and his teacher was aware of his diagnosis. Recently Camden came to school and was disoriented, weak, and cranky. Concerned about low blood sugar, she had him escorted to the school office, and he then passed out. As this condition can be fatal, Camden had to be rushed to the hospital and given treatment. It took awhile to locate Denise, and when she came to the hospital she was irritated that this had happened. She complained to the hospital social worker that she just couldn't keep up with Camden and his requirements for treatment and that he had brought this on himself due to his not eating breakfast. She thought it was Paul's fault too as it is his job to make sure Camden eats. Denise stated that this had happened twice before (getting low blood sugar), and all people need to do is give him some juice. Due to Denise's lack of recognition of the gravity of the situation, her expectations of maturity beyond a 5-year-old level for Camden (and for 7-year-old Paul), and her lack of responsibility for his medical needs, the social worker filed a report with CPS regarding medical neglect. After an initial investigation, Denise agreed to work with a social worker, who specializes in medical neglect, without a court order to do so. In this example, the CPS social worker assigned to Denise's case is meeting with her for the first time.

The following dialogue is written in an abbreviated format of a process recording, which is a method of social work education that is used to examine client–social worker dialogue as well as to determine what the social worker was thinking of or felt during the interview. In this vignette, the social worker has written his internal monologue: how he reacted to the client, the cognitive messages he told himself in order to express empathy, and the empathic resonation that he experienced while talking to Denise, the client.

Once again, we code the interactions using the following:

- GI = giving information
- SR = simple reflection
- CR = complex reflection
- OQ = open-ended question
- CQ = closed-ended question

- MIA = MI adherent (affirming, asking permission, emphasizing personal control, support)

Actual Dialogue	*Internal Monologue of the Social Worker*
SOCIAL WORKER: Hi, Denise, my name is Lawrence Taylor and I will be working with you, as I explained on the phone. How are you doing today [OQ]?	
CLIENT: Oh, OK, I guess. I think that social worker at the hospital really over-reacted as have you people [from CPS]. It was my son's fault that his blood sugar went low. I mean he looked fine to me when I took him to school. I had given him his shot. I can't be watching everything he does. He should've eaten his breakfast like he knows he is supposed to do.	*Yikes! She is still blaming him for this problem. Don't get caught up in this. Focus on what she is saying.*
SOCIAL WORKER: If Camden had done what he was supposed to do, you wouldn't be here talking to me now [CR].	
CLIENT: Yes, he knows that he has to have carbs after he gets his	

shot. I have a 7-year-old too, and I can't watch Cam every minute. I told him, explained to him, what he needs to do to take care of himself. Getting them both out of the door in the morning is crazy. I gave him his shot—that takes time we don't have in the morning—and I was also busy with making sure Paul had his homework with him. Paul was supposed to make sure he ate. Don't worry, I'm doing it *all* now.

SOCIAL WORKER: Things are difficult and hectic for you in the mornings, especially with having to do it all yourself. It helps if the kids take on some responsibilities and since the ER visit, you are handling Cam's diabetes [CR].

She has a lot to do, on her own. Let her know that I understand this. Come alongside, even if her expectations are unrealistic.

CLIENT: Yes, my husband is gone and won't be back for awhile. And then he will probably be deployed again so I have to manage. It's hard to do everything myself.

SOCIAL WORKER: You carry a lot of responsibility [SR].

Use as many reflections as possible, to help engage her and learn what she is thinking.

CLIENT: You are right about that! I knew what I was getting into when I got married and with him being in the Navy. But I never in a million years dreamed I would have a kid with medical problems! What about *me*? What about *my* life? I want to relax a little, have fun, not worry about carbs, shots, blood sugars, doctors. I sure didn't sign on for this.

What about Cam? He didn't ask for diabetes either! Telling her this will only create an argument and not engage her.

SOCIAL WORKER: Camden's diabetes is very difficult to care for, and you had no idea how hard this was going to be. You feel a bit cheated [CR].

Hypothesis-test that she feels cheated.

CLIENT: Cheated is right! I had plans for when the kids got older, got in school. I want to go back to school. I want to be somebody myself. Don't get me wrong, I love my kids, but I also want to work on my needs and doing what I want. And now you people think I should go to a *parenting* class? I *know* how to be a parent. Look at me! I manage two kids on my own, no husband or family around to help, and a sick kid to boot. You all think I need to *learn* more?

But the parenting class will help her learn about child development and what is realistic. Yes, she needs to learn more. But my telling her this won't help. Focus on what she is trying to tell me. She feels burdened by having another requirement in her life.

SOCIAL WORKER: Going to a parenting class wasn't what you had in mind of how to spend your time. You have been working hard to manage Cam's illness, and this feels like one more expectation on top of it [CR].

CLIENT: I agreed to do it, but I think it is stupid.

Telling her it's not stupid will only start an argument.

SOCIAL WORKER: How would you like to spend the time together that we have today? You have a lot on your plate. How can I be of help to you [OQ]?

Begin to guide the conversation.

CLIENT: (*Sighs.*) There's nothing you can do to help me. I am in this alone. I have been doing everything myself. So I made one little mistake. Cam told me that he ate! Do I have to check him every time?

SOCIAL WORKER: So one of the things we could talk about today is how you manage Cam's diabetes without any assistance, or we could talk about your own goals or about anything else you have in mind. It is up to you [MIA].

CLIENT: Well, I think I manage the diabetes pretty well. But it is not just up to me to manage it! He has to eat when he should, and he should tell me when he feels low [blood sugar]. He needs to tell other people too, like his teacher. He just is so stubborn. He gets mad sometimes when I have to give him a shot and runs away from me and hides. I don't have time to be chasing him all over the house! He knows he needs it, like it or not.

SOCIAL WORKER: So not only are you feeling overwhelmed by this but Cam is too. When he won't cooperate, it makes it even worse for you [CR].

CLIENT: Yes, I know I lose my temper with him but sometimes the only thing that works is for me to yell at him. Then he cries and gets even more upset, but at least I get the shot in. I tell him, "You *have* to do this! Do you think I *like* doing it?"

SOCIAL WORKER: So you both hate it. One way you try to manage how upset Cam is, is to yell at

---

Yes, she should always check. I need to engage her more before I offer any education. Plus she'll get a lot of information at a parent support group.

Let's try some more guiding again to get a focus. Make sure to support her autonomy.

His behavior is pretty typical for a 5-year-old, and she should expect this. Telling her this won't help right now. Focus on what she is saying as well as what is going on with Cam.

They both are having such a hard time with this.

Let's see what she can tell me about what she does do well instead of focusing on the negatives.

him and then you find that it just makes things worse, at least emotionally, and you know he got his insulin [CR]. How else do you manage his diabetes [OQ]?

CLIENT: Well, I do try to buy the right foods, but it is hard when Paul starts telling me he wants certain snacks or some of his Halloween candy that I have to hide to keep Cam away from it. I put food he can have at his level where he can get to it and keep the other stuff up high.

SOCIAL WORKER: You make sure Cam is eating the right foods. How else do you manage the diabetes [OQ]?

Keep asking her to list what she is doing to manage the diabetes.

CLIENT: I get up most nights to check his sugar. But I can't always do it. Can *you* imagine never being able to sleep through the night, *ever*? So I say I get up three out of seven nights. I am just too tired to do it every single night. He's never had a problem unless he doesn't eat right that evening.

This is really hard on parents, to have to check levels every night, especially when they have no one to help them.

SOCIAL WORKER: And on the nights when you check his sugar, why do you do that [OQ]?

CLIENT: Well, I'm not always sure what he ate, and if he went into a coma while we were both asleep … that would be bad. I don't want him to die.

SOCIAL WORKER: You make sure he gets his shots, you keep the right foods in the house, and you check

Summarize and keep asking for more positive coping.

his blood levels most nights [SR].
What else do you do [OQ]?

CLIENT: I don't know. We go for
walks. I take him to soccer.
He gets exercise. He's a kid;
he's running around all day
anyway.

SOCIAL WORKER: So you work at
managing his diabetes, and you
are doing this on your own. You
check his insulin levels and give
him the shots, even when he fights
it; you buy the right kinds of food
and have them available to him;
most nights you are monitoring
him; and you go for walks and
get him into some sports activities
[SR—summary].

*A summary will help reinforce
what she is doing right and hopefully keep those behaviors going.*

CLIENT: Yeah, that would be about
right. I get tired just hearing it.

*Acknowledge how hard this is for
her.*

SOCIAL WORKER: You're really trying to be a good mother and take
care of him [MIA]. You find it
overwhelming even though you
are working to do the right things
[CR].

CLIENT: Yes. It's hard.

SOCIAL WORKER: Can I ask, when
you first started working with
your doctor, when Camden was
diagnosed, what did they tell
you about parent support groups
[OQ]?

*Elicit from her what she knows
already.*

CLIENT: Oh, I don't know, they may
have mentioned it. I just didn't
think it would make any difference. I mean, how would it
change what I am dealing with?

SOCIAL WORKER: Would it be OK with you if I gave you some information about support groups [MIA]? Many of the things you talked about are common feelings among parents who have children with diabetes. Some of the parents I have worked with find that going to a support group is really helpful. You could be with other parents who have to deal with similar situations, such as when your child runs away from you when it is time for a shot, or cries, or eats the wrong foods. They can tell you how they handled certain problems, and you could share your ways that work as well. It is different from a parenting class as it is only led by parents for parents. And you would know that you're not alone [GI]. What do you think of this [OQ]?

Support her autonomy by asking permission. Provide her some information about support groups. Use some of the concerns that she has already stated.

Elicit what she thinks of this.

CLIENT: Well, I could try it. At least it couldn't hurt. Is it free? How long is it?

SOCIAL WORKER: (*Provides details.*)

CLIENT: OK, I will give that a try. Maybe I could get some good advice and at least talk to other people who understand *me* and what I am going through.

The support group may help her not feel so alone and isolated and will provide some good diabetes management info too. I'm glad she is open to going. I feel like we have started to engage in a working relationship.

SOCIAL WORKER: Great, maybe we can talk about your experience with it when I see you next week. Before I go, when you said you are you are doing it "all" now, what did you mean [OQ]?

I need to check in regarding safety issues and see what she meant.

CLIENT: I am testing and making sure he eats in the morning and at night. I don't want to go through this again, as hard as it is to have to do everything.

SOCIAL WORKER: You are monitoring Cam's levels and his eating several times a day [CR].

CLIENT: Yes, it isn't easy, but I am doing it. Maybe I can get some moral support at that support group.

SOCIAL WORKER: It will be helpful to talk to others in the same situation [CR].

DISCUSSION

The social worker in this vignette approached this interview with a goal of engaging Denise and getting her connected to some support and parenting classes. He also needed to monitor the situation for Cam's safety.

The focus of this interview was to express empathy in order to engage with this client; it was very tempting for the social worker to launch into warning, advising, or trying to educate Denise, as noted by his internal monologue. Doing so, however, would not only have kept him from facilitating some open communication with Denise; advice or threats would have caused Denise to become resistant and tune him out. As hard as it was for him to reflect what she was saying, he did so without agreeing with her or "cushioning" his statements. He resisted the righting reflex through coming alongside. The social worker experienced empathic resonation and was able to communicate to Denise how hard dealing with this disease was for both her and her son. With a focus on what she is doing well (or somewhat well) to manage the diabetes, Denise felt heard, affirmed, and free to disclose the difficulties she is experiencing. She discussed more than what she might have otherwise, if the social worker had immediately started challenging her or warning her.

The social worker guided Denise to set an agenda of what she wanted to discuss during their time together, providing a direction for the MI interview. Denise somewhat resisted this as she was feeling so overwhelmed with a variety of concerns. The social worker reflected her role in providing for Cam alone as well as her own goals as possible things they could discuss. He supported her autonomy to choose the direction of the interview, although he knew that at some point he would have to discuss safety issues regarding Cam. The social worker did this at the end of the interview after he had engaged Denise by listening to her ambivalence and providing support for her. He knew that if she were willing to attend both parenting classes and the support group, this would help her increase her knowledge and hopefully impact her behavior regarding the care of her children. The social worker waited until the end of the interview to address safety issues when she was most comfortable and would be most honest with him.

FINAL THOUGHTS

Reflective listening is a key skill in MI and should be used twice or three times as often as questions, if we want to engage our clients and learn what they are experiencing and/or thinking (Miller & Rollnick, 2002). Doing so keeps us focused on the immediacy of our clients' words, not thinking ahead to the next question we want to ask or the information we need to collect. Interestingly, while there is no research evidence on this topic, anecdotal stories have described how using MI spirit and expressing empathy have actually reduced burnout among social workers, who no longer feel the need to advise, threaten, or warn clients. Yes, there are times when we do have to share the outcomes or consequences of behavior; in MI this is done in a way that supports clients' autonomy, and we don't feel the need to be the one to personally make them change. Working to express empathy takes us out of the "expert" role and into the role of the listener, even in situations when it is very difficult to hear what clients might be saying.

6

Developing Discrepancy

Using Motivational Interviewing
in a Group Setting to Increase Ambivalence

There is a story in my husband's family about the time his elderly father went to the doctor for a check-up. The doctor told him that he had to lose weight to reduce his blood pressure. His response was, "How much do I have to lose?" The doctor told him 20 to 25 pounds and handed him a diet. In his usual determined style, he went out and promptly lost 25 pounds. Unfortunately, brief physician advice like this is not always followed (Tsai & Wadden, 2009), even in the face of current or pending health consequences. In Chapter 4, we presented an example of someone for whom change was important but who lacked confidence that she could do it. In the example of my father-in-law, losing weight was important, as his doctor had told him that he had to do it for health reasons; he was also confident and committed to changing his eating patterns. In this chapter, we will consider the situation of where there is low importance: clients who know that perhaps changes need to be made but to make the change is just not that important. For other clients we sometimes work with, making a change is not even on their radar.

In order to increase ambivalence or the salience of a concern to a client, we can use strategies to develop discrepancy. As we discussed in Chapter 2, developing discrepancy was an early concept in MI and was based on Festinger's (1957) dissonance theory. In this theory, humans have certain values and goals, or motivators, and being out of sync between our "ideal selves" and our "current selves" can create discomfort. When the discrepancy or discomfort is great enough, we are ready to make changes. Speaking about change out loud causes us to think about it, perhaps in ways we haven't done in the past (self-perception theory; Bem, 1972). According to Miller and Rollnick (2002), "In MI, eliciting change talk is a primary method for developing discrepancy" (p. 83). Using methods to elicit change talk can create an increase or a shift in our clients' ambivalence, particularly if the problem under discussion has been fairly unimportant. The change comes from clients' own thinking and discussion of the issue. My father-in-law is a rare example of someone whose behavior changed based on the advice of someone else; most people need to "hear themselves think" and listen to their own advice. If we can help them do this in an autonomous-supportive manner, clients are more likely to make a shift.

How do we know if change under discussion is important to our clients? One way is to ask them. Using a change ruler question, we can say, "On a scale of 0 to 10, with 0 being 'not important at all' and 10 being 'extremely important', how important is it for you to ... ?" But before we even ask the importance question, we can possibly learn of our clients' perspectives by listening for their *change talk*. We want to hear about the ambivalence they may already have. As described in Chapter 2, change talk is any discussion of the *desire, ability, reasons, need* (preparatory language), and *commitment or taking steps* (commitment language) (another mnemonic: DARN-CaT) to change (Amrhein, 2004; Amrhein, Miller, Yahne, Palmer, & Fulcher, 2003). The following are some brief examples of what we want to listen for:

- *Desire to change:*
  - "I want to be a better parent for my son."
  - "I wish things could be different."

- *Ability to change:*
  - "I can do it; I was able to quit smoking before."
  - "When I put my mind to something, I get determined."

- *Reasons for change:*
  - "If I want to keep the courts off my back, then I need to follow my probation."
  - "If I come to school every day, then my grades will go up."

- *Need for change:*
  - "I need for things to be different."
  - "I have got to get a job."

- *Commitment:*
  - "I will call that treatment program tomorrow."
  - "I'll try to see my doctor next week."
  - "I guarantee that you will see me do things differently this time."

- *Taking steps:*
  - "I applied for three jobs this week."
  - "I threw out all of my drug paraphernalia."

There is a DARN-CaT equivalent for sustain talk as well. This includes statements in support of the status quo, such as when clients tell us why they shouldn't, can't, don't need or want to change or tell us why certain behaviors are not a problem.

WHY CHANGE TALK IS "GOLD"

Miller and Moyers (2006) emphasize that it is important to recognize and respond to change talk when we hear it, perhaps even before we work to elicit it. Living in California, I often use the metaphor of listening for DARN-CaT talk is like panning for gold (yes, some people still actually do it!). We pay attention to change talk and respond to it in order to highlight it and guide the conversation in a particular direction. We let the "silt and sand" of the rest of the conversation filter through and focus on the "nuggets."

Research is now supporting the idea that change talk is "gold." A causal model proposed by Miller and Rose (2009) shows that both counselor empathy and MI technical skill are predictive of client change talk (preparatory language). This in turn leads to commitment language, which then ultimately predicts outcome. The strength of commitment language is particularly important ("I will ... " as compared to "I might ... ") (Amrhein et al., 2003). In studies of clients with alcohol use disorders, sustain talk by clients was related to no change in drinking habits at follow-up, while change talk during counseling sessions was related to decreased drinking (Apodaca & Longabaugh, 2009; Baer et al., 2008; Moyers, Martin, et al., 2007; Moyers et al., 2009; Vader, Walters, Prabhu, Houch, & Field, 2010). Thus, in using MI we focus particularly on listening for change talk, and we respond to it by using reflections and other MI methods. Practitioner behaviors that are consistent with MI have been demonstrated to increase change talk (Catley et al., 2006; Glynn & Moyers, 2010). "What therapists reflect, they will hear more of" (Moyers et al., 2009, p. 1122).

STRATEGIC USE OF METHODS TO ENCOURAGE OR ELICIT CHANGE TALK

Responding to Change Talk When We Hear It

Consider the following statements from a client who is an elderly woman. She is discussing with the social worker at her senior center a conversation that she recently had with her children. They want her to give up her driver's license. The change talk is in **bold.**

> "My kids have been telling me that I should stop driving, but I think they are exaggerating. **I know I'll need to quit eventually** [need], but I haven't had an accident in over 30 years! **I did get a scare the other day backing out in a parking lot and almost hitting another car** [reason], but that can happen to anybody. **I just can't turn around and look like I used to** [(in)ability]. I'm extra careful when I drive, though, and **I don't drive at night anymore** [taking steps]. I mean, **I would never want to hurt anybody** [desire], but I just think it's too soon to give up my license. If I did, I'd be depending on them all the time, and I don't want to do that. **I guess I could get rides in the senior van** [ability]. I appreciate that they are concerned about me, but I really don't want to give up driving yet."

How we respond to change talk when we hear it is important, otherwise it is lost gold. Using the EARS mnemonic, we can go in several different directions. We can use (E) elaboration questions, such as "Tell me more about. . . . " or "What happens when . . . ?" or "Why . . . ?"; (A) affirmations; (R) reflections; and/or (S) a summary (see Chapter 2 for definitions). Beginning MI learners sometimes use the skills correctly, but what they choose to focus on guides the client in the direction of continuing to discuss the status quo (sustain talk). Just as clients will utilize sustain and change talk, it is easy for us to get caught in the "silt and sand" and focus on that in our responses and let the gold nuggets just fall out of mining pan.

Although it is impossible to know how clients might respond, think about how what is emphasized might encourage either more change talk or sustain talk. Remember, increased change talk is related to actual change. Here are some examples of using EARS in response to the above client statement that could either elicit more sustain talk or change talk.

E (elaboration): "Why do you think that they are so far off base?" [→ sustain talk]
"What made you stop driving at night?" [→ change talk]
"What are the reasons your children brought this up?" [→ change talk]

A (affirmation): "You really value your independence." [→ sustain talk]
"You would never want to accidentally hurt anyone." [→ change talk]

R (reflection): "The fact that your children would bring this up is really puzzling to you." [→ sustain talk]
"Your children are really concerned about your welfare." [→ change talk]

S (summary): "Your children think you should give up your license, and you think they are off base. You almost had an accident, but this had nothing to do with your driving skills. It was just one of those fluke things. You will know when you are ready to quit driving." [→ sustain talk]
"Your children have approached you about giving up your license. While you are puzzled by this, you also want to avoid ever hurting anyone. You are worried about being dependent on them, and you also know that your children are only saying this because they are concerned about you." [→ change talk; describe the client's ambivalence]

All of these examples are demonstrations of the EARS responses to either sustain talk or change talk from the client. We know we have picked the wrong area to reflect or ask about when it brings up more sustain talk and some of the statements or questions above could lead the client to further discuss what a crazy idea her children have and how her children are completely wrong. The other questions/statements could elicit change talk regarding the reasons or her desire to not hurt anyone. Reflecting sustain talk can be done strategically to roll with resistance and engage with our clients, as is discussed in Chapter 7. In MI, though, we want to guide the conversation forward as much as possible, particularly when clients are already giving us some "gold."

Eliciting Change Talk When It Doesn't Come Up in Conversation

Consider another client. He is a man in his early 30s who has been convicted of driving under the influence (DUI) and is required to attend group counseling at a local DUI program. He is meeting with his counselor for an individual session:

> "I've been coming to these group sessions for awhile but I can tell you, I am not like these other people in my group. *They* really have problems with their drinking. I mean **I learned my lesson with the drinking and driving thing** [possible commitment or taking steps], but all this talk about having drinking problems and needing to go to AA and to quit drinking, why that just doesn't fit my situation. I like to drink, I can handle drinking, and I know when to stop. My drinking is not causing me problems. I have a good job, a good apartment, and a girlfriend, who by the way, thinks that this whole thing is overkill for me, to have to come here. Don't get me wrong, you are a great counselor and all, but this all so ridiculous. I'm fine."

Well! Here is a client with little to no ambivalence about his behavior under consideration. How do we use EARS with this situation? If we do, all we end up doing is reflecting sustain talk, as this client is not even somewhat worried, as was the elderly client in the previous situation. He has no concerns about his alcohol use and thus finds it totally unimportant to change. Is using EARS here a problem?

This type of scenario is not unusual with clients whom we might encounter in situations where they are mandated or court-ordered to receive our services. It isn't their idea to change; it is someone else's. In these settings, as social workers we have a couple of tasks. One is to assume that there is ambivalence that is buried underneath the "reactance" (the push-back: "I'm fine, leave me alone") we hear from clients (Miller & Rollnick, 2002). All the sustain talk can be a result of having autonomy threatened. If client-centered theory tells us that humans are driven toward health and positive growth (Rogers, 1959), situations that cause clients to not experience this might give them a little pause, at least somewhere in their thinking. We need to create an open environment or atmosphere that allows them to move past the reactance and to begin to consider that maybe there is a concern that they have, underneath it all. Beyond using EARS, we can provide safe space through use of rolling with resistance strategies, as presented in Chapter 7, as they work with sustain talk as well. Clients who are not pressured to change may be more willing to examine the behavior under discussion (Wagner & Ingersoll, in press). Eliciting change talk strategies is helpful and is particularly useful once we have established rapport and engagement with our clients and have moved them into a place where they feel safe to explore concerns.

There are several different strategies for evoking change talk that include elaboration, or asking clients to explain more or give more detail; looking forward or asking about what the future would be like should clients make the change under discussion; looking backward or asking clients to talk about a time when the behavior was not a problem or issue; asking what might be the best thing about making a change. These latter three methods all work to help clients envision how life might be different or better (Miller & Rollnick, 2002; Rosengren, 2009). The following are some examples of eliciting change talk strategies that work particularly well with those who have little to no ambivalence. We have examined the change ruler already, but it presented again to demonstrate how it can be used to assess importance of a goal, value, or behavior.

Change Ruler

In our example of the change ruler in Chapter 4, the social worker asked about both the importance of change and the client's confidence in changing. Again, in using the change ruler, we usually ask, "How important is it for you to __ on a scale of 0, not important at all, to 10, very important?" This is followed up by questions that encourage change talk: "Why are you a __ and not a __ [lower number]? What would it take for you to go from [lower number] to [slightly higher number]?" Often the answers to these will provide reason change talk. Asking the same question, regarding the client's confidence, will give us the ability to change talk (Miller & Rollnick, 2002). Summarizing the responses back to clients helps pull together the discussion, and they hear themselves think out loud.

Sometimes the target behavior for the change ruler may be discovered in discussion with clients around their values or things that motivate them. For instance, with our elderly client, while the topic was the decision to give up her driver's license, the change ruler could be asked regarding how important it was for her to not endanger anyone else or to remain independent. Most likely both of these alternatives are important; then her confidence to remain safe on the road, or to be independent even without a license, could be explored.

In our DUI client's situation, if he was asked how important it would be to change his drinking, he would probably say a 1 or a 2, not very important. Asking him what it might take to make it more important to him, he might say if he got another DUI, or had health issues, or his girl-friend left him over his drinking. Then his confidence would be explored, and he could be asked that if he *were* to modify his drinking, how would he rate his ability to do that? Since he doesn't see it as a problem, he would most likely be very confident that he could make changes. His counselor could summarize this all back to him:

> "Right now you rate the importance of changing your drinking as low, but it would become more important should you get another DUI, have health issues, or have your girlfriend get angry with you over it. And you know that since you have quit smoking, that if you chose to modify or change your drinking, you would be fairly confident that you could do it."

For the client who has little to no ambivalence, a discussion such as this might help to raise it a bit.

Decisional Balance

The decisional balance is a structured exercise to weigh out both the pros and cons of changing a behavior or not changing it (Miller, 2004; Miller & Rollnick, 2002). Sometimes it is drawn in a diagram of four squares, and clients are asked to consider each section and write them in. Our elderly client might be asked, "What would be the benefits of continuing to drive? What would be the negatives or downside of continuing to drive? What would be the downside of not driving anymore? What would be the benefits of not driving anymore?" The social worker then reflects these answers back to the client in a summary, using an "and" between them all. This gives clients a chance to examine all sides of their ambivalence that can exist simultaneously. If there is a direction in the interview, then we would end our summary with the change talk that we want our clients to hear last. They are hearing their own words, out loud.

In more recent years, in MI there has been a move away from the decisional balance, for according to Miller and Rollnick (2009), in using this tool, we are going on "a hunt for sustain talk" (p. 133). They emphasize that it is better to focus on change talk and selectively reinforce that as much as possible, for as research shows this is where real movement occurs. The decisional balance is best used where there is equipoise or where we are "consciously nondirective" in the discussion (Miller & Rollnick, 2002, p. 96). In our elderly client instance, the social worker may have no indication that the client is a dangerous driver. Her goal in using a decisional balance is to help her client decide for herself what the best course of action might be.

Values Exploration

Social work education is typically rich with emphasis on the values and ethics of the profession, and most of us are quite familiar with those advocated by the National Association of Social Workers. Values have been defined as "what is good and desirable" (Dolgoff, Loewenberg, & Harrington, 2005, p. 18). They have also been called "behavioral ideals or preferences for experiences" (Wagner & Sanchez, 2002, p. 285). While as social workers we hold similar values and know what they are, there is a diversity of values held by humans. We just don't often stop and take stock of what our values are and how we measure up to them. Doing so can be an impetus to change (Wagner & Sanchez, 2002).

Recently in an interview in the *Los Angeles Times*, Deepak Chopra, writer and healer, was asked about New Year's resolutions. His response was:

> I'm not saying everybody should do it, but even if you took five, 10 minutes of quiet time every day or every other day or once a week and asked yourself simple questions like, who am I? What do I want? What is my life's purpose? Is there a contribution I can make to my community or to society? What kind of relationships do I want to have? What is my idea of well being, and how can I achieve it? I don't ask that you even know the answers, but if you start to do this kind of reflection, it has a very interesting way of not only moving you to the answers but of changing your behavior. (in Lacher, 2010, p. D3)

The values card sort (VCS) exercise was created by Miller, C'de Baca, Matthews, and Wilbourne (2001) as a way to help clients reflect on their values, in much the same manner that Chopra advocates. It is especially well suited for those with little to no ambivalence, as the focus initially is more on what is important to clients and away from discussions of the target behavior. Analyzing values and the distance clients may be from them can help to develop discrepancy.

The VCS can be found at *casaa.unm.edu/inst/Personal%20Values%20 Card%20Sort.pdf*, along with instructions on how to use it. It is a list of 83 values that can be cut up into small cards. Examples of the values include acceptance, achievement, compassion, excitement, fame, friendship, health, intimacy, purpose, self-acceptance, and wealth. While there are many variations on how to use the cards, ask clients to sort through the cards and make five piles: those that are "least important to me," "not important to me," "neither important or unimportant to me," "somewhat important to me," and "important to me." The "most important" pile is limited to 10 cards. Next, have clients go through the "most important" and discuss what each card (value) means to them. Ask how clients are living the value, with plenty of reflections as they are discussed. Clients can then be asked how they are not living the value and what is getting in the way, and/or what the relationship is between the values and the target behavior (Rosengren, 2009). In this instance, our DUI client could be asked how drinking impacts the values he has selected. Our role is to provide reflections and summaries throughout the process.

MI IN GROUP SETTINGS

Because the example of developing discrepancy that is given next is applied in a group setting, it is helpful to take a brief overview of MI in this context. Over the past decade or so, MI has been applied to group work with some good outcomes. As group therapy is so prevalent in substance use treatment, most of the applications have been adolescents, college students, or adults, all with alcohol or drug-related concerns, but it has been used in other settings as well. Often called group MI or GMI, group sessions may be manualized with specific topics and exercises, and groups may be offered once, twice, four, or up to 10 times, depending on the study (Engle, Macgowen, Wagner, & Amrheim, 2010; Foote et al., 1999; Ingersoll, Wagner, & Gharib, 2002; LaChance, Ewing, Bryan, & Hutchison, 2009; Lincourt, Kuettel, & Bombardier, 2002; Santa Ana, Wulfert, & Nietert, 2007; Velasquez, Maurer, Crouch, & DiClemente, 2001). MI groups can also be process-focused where they are not manualized and are unstructured (Wagner & Ingersoll, in press).

Due to the history of confrontational methods in substance use treatment, clients who participate in an MI-based group often expect a GMI intervention to be more of the same. Because it is difficult to attend to group processes and to reinforce a different way of interacting, those who want to use this format should be proficient in both group work and in MI in order to combine the two effectively (Wagner & Ingersoll, in press). One of the first tasks of the group leader is to indicate that the GMI is different from what clients may be expecting and to set the tone of the MI spirit of collaboration, autonomy support, and empathy. This is often done through modeling of MI interactions as well as by redirecting and reframing negative or confrontational comments or unsolicited advice that may arise from group members (Ingersoll et al., 2002; Velasquez, Stephens, & Ingersoll, 2006). Group members may be taught how to utilize simple reflective listening methods to further integrate MI into the group process (Rose & Chang, 2010; Velasquez et al., 2006).

Empathy is a key ingredient in GMI. Reflective listening that is used selectively helps to demonstrate this as well as reinforce change talk as it occurs in the group setting. While it is important to acknowledge sustain talk and the ambivalence that clients struggle with, those using GMI work to focus on positives as a way to move forward and not get stuck in the past. As indicated earlier, developing discrepancy is used in a framework of optimism—for group members to think about ways to improve lives and live more closely with their desired values and goals. It is a "taste" of possibilities that the future could hold (Wagner & Ingersoll, in press).

DEVELOPING DISCREPANCY IN A GROUP SETTING: EXAMPLE AND DIALOGUE

The DUI client who was described above is fairly typical of clients sentenced to DUI programs. Most are young adult males who are single but employed. Their alcohol-related problems may not be as extensive as alcohol- or substance-dependent clients seen in traditional treatment programs, but at least 50 to 90% qualify for a lifetime alcohol use disorder diagnosis (Cavaiolo & Wuth, 2002; Lapham et al., 2001). Most are required to attend some sort of counseling program, which usually involves education, group work with an approved curriculum, and individual counseling as well as AA (Alcoholics Anonymous) meetings in the community. Many come to the DUI programs feeling very committed to not drinking and driving again, but fewer believe there is a need to modify their drinking.

As long as they don't drink and drive, they think, there is no problem. The goals of DUI programs are to decrease both further DUI and alcohol-related problems, thus the emphasis on examining the impacts of alcohol in all aspects of clients' lives (Cavaiolo & Wuth, 2002). In the following example, a social worker, who is leading a group of about 10 DUI clients, uses a values card sort exercise.

Once again, we will code the interactions using the following:

• GI = giving information • SR = simple reflection • CR = complex reflection • OQ = open-ended question • CQ = closed-ended question   • MIA = MI adherent (affirming, asking permission, emphasizing personal control, support)

SOCIAL WORKER: [Has already done opening and check-in with the group.] Our group today will focus on our values, or things that are really important to us. I am going to give you each a stack of cards that list all kinds of values. There are even two blanks if you want to write one of your own. (*Hands out the cards.*) If you would, please go through these and make five piles. [GI—request] (*Explains, as above.*)

[Group starts sorting through them. Some use their laps; others make their piles on the floor. There is high energy in the room as they take on the task.]

CLIENT 1: Whoa, this is a lot. How do you ever decide?

CLIENT 2: What if most of them are important?

SOCIAL WORKER: It can be a bit overwhelming with so many [CR].
          [After group is done:]

SOCIAL WORKER: Next, the second step is a little harder. Please take the cards from your "Most important to me pile" and pick out your top 10 [GI].

[Group continues to sort through and create new piles.]

CLIENT 3: This is even worse than the first step!

SOCIAL WORKER: Everyone done? Please take your top 10 "most important" cards. If you are willing [MIA], please present these to the group. Tell us what your values are and what each individual value means to you [OQ].

CLIENT 1: OK, I'll go first. I picked "family." I have three kids and a wife, and they mean everything to me. I also picked "health." If you don't have your health, you are in big trouble. I picked "independence" because I don't like anyone telling me what to do, nor do I want to have to depend on anyone for work. I need to be able to take care of my own family. I picked "achievement" because it is important for me to be a success and be independent. I picked "acceptance" because I feel like it is important for me to accept myself and other people.

SOCIAL WORKER: Thank you, [Client 1], that is terrific [MIA]. Who else would like to share [OQ]?

CLIENT 4: Well, I picked some different ones, but I agree with you, [Client 1]. A lot of those are really important. It was really hard to pick! I picked "family" too. I hang out with my brothers a lot, they are really like my best friends. I picked "leisure" as we like to all go to the river and ski. That is the best time, when we are all just together, me with my brothers. "Fitness" is really important to me, to be in shape. I picked "wealth" because, who doesn't want money? It would be nice to not to have to worry about it. I also picked "humor" as everyone enjoys someone with a good sense of humor.

[Several others share their own.]

SOCIAL WORKER: I really appreciate how many of you have shared [MIA]. I—and probably the rest of the group—have learned a few new things about everyone [GI]!

CLIENT 5: I learned a few things about myself that I didn't really realize before this.

SOCIAL WORKER: What did you learn [OQ]?

CLIENT 5: Well, I picked "stability." I never would've guessed that. But looking at the cards, this was one that was "most important." I guess it's because I don't like change. I like to know how my life is going to be every day, ya know? That I have a job. I have a place to live. I don't have to worry about what I am going to eat. I feel like I am describing my dad, not me. But here I am.

SOCIAL WORKER: Thank you for sharing that [MIA]. You found out that there is something to you, deep down, that you didn't know was there before [CR]. It's funny how just looking through and having to choose from these cards can make us look at things in a different way [GI].

CLIENT 1: Yeah, [Client 5], who would have guessed? You act like you're this big drinker who likes to go out and party all of the time.

CLIENT 5: Well, I still like to drink! As long as my bar stays the same! Seriously, do you think I can be "stable" and still party? It does seem funny.

SOCIAL WORKER: Well, now that you ask this, I would like to ask you all to go back to your "most important" pile and take a look at how alcohol and your values go together. How does drinking impact how you live out your values [OQ]?

CLIENT 2: You want us to go back and describe each one again?

SOCIAL WORKER: Yes [GI], that would be great [MIA].

CLIENT 4: "Family": hmmm. Well, when I drink, I fit in with my family. All of my brothers love to drink, like when we go to the river, or to a football game. It's what we do. I mean, when I told them I had to go to AA for this DUI, they really laughed. They told me, "Have fun with that one." My old man died of a stroke when he was a little older than me. He probably was an alcoholic. Sometimes I wonder where this is all going to go for us. "Leisure": well, that would be all the fun we have together. I love to water ski. Not such a good idea when you're loaded though! "Fitness": Well, it is definitely hard to stay fit when you have a beer belly! "Wealth": I'd love to have it, but I don't work on it too well.

CLIENT 1: What do you spend a week on alcohol?

CLIENT 4: Probably about $100 a week or more. I don't know. Maybe if I cut back I could save some money. My last value was "humor": well, when I get drunk everyone seems to think it is funny. So alcohol helps me in that case to be more outgoing and funny.

SOCIAL WORKER: On the one hand, alcohol helps you fit in with your family, especially when it comes to being funny, and on the other hand, you worry about how it might affect your health and that of your brothers. It also makes it hard to do physical activities and stay in shape due to all the calories, and it's expensive [CR—double sided reflection].

CLIENT 4: I never thought of it that way. I just can't imagine being with my brothers and not drinking so much. They would really think something was wrong with me.

CLIENT 3: Maybe if you told them that you didn't want to die young like your dad, they would understand. Maybe they would cut back too.

CLIENT 4: Maybe …

SOCIAL WORKER: [Client 3] is trying to be helpful, to think of some ideas of how to handle this [SR]. Only you, [Client 4], can decide if you want to say anything to your brothers or do anything about your drinking and if you do, the best way to do this [MIA—autonomy support].

CLIENT 4: Well thanks, I appreciate your help, [Client 3].

CLIENT 1: I'll go next. "Family": well, my wife was sure mad at me for the DUI. She gets mad when I come home after drinking. My kids don't like it much either. Usually I just fall asleep. They go to bed and leave me sitting in my chair. "Health": I know drinking isn't good for your health, but so far so good for me. Other than the calories. "Independence": I run my own business so I am independent. I don't drink on the job. Sometimes I am hung over but I don't think my employees notice. "Achievement": We were poor growing up so I want to make sure we don't have money problems. Drinking—well, it does cost money. But I always put my company first and work as hard as I can. "Acceptance": I don't accept myself too much for this DUI, I can honestly say that. When I drink too much, it makes it hard to do.

CLIENT 5: I said "stability," much to my surprise. Yes, I would say alcohol affects that, especially when you have to sleep in jail overnight. My other values were a lot like the rest of yours—family, work, health. Even though I didn't think I had an alcohol problem, doing the card thing has made me look at it all a bit differently. My girlfriend is important to me, but she has threatened to break up with me if I get in trouble again. She says she won't be with a "drunk"—that she had enough of that with her ex.

SOCIAL WORKER: Stability is important to her as well; she wants someone she can count on [CR].

CLIENT 5: Yes, I think that is true.

SOCIAL WORKER: So one of the themes that we seem to be hearing is that while we all have these wonderful values that truly define who we are, many times alcohol use really gets in the way of living them out. Thinking about our values makes us think about ourselves and where we are in our lives. Alcohol helps some of the values and also causes problems with them [CR—summary].

CLIENT 5: Yeah, I need to think about all of this. Maybe I should cut back my drinking.

DISCUSSION

In this group, the social worker had several tasks. One was for her to structure the VCS exercise for the clients. She had to attend to group processes as well as demonstrate MI spirit and utilize MI skills. She intervened when a group member tried to give another member unsolicited advice by reminding the client that it was ultimately up to him to make the decisions regarding his drinking. She also had to pull together the common themes that came up in the group that each member could relate to (Velasquez et al., 2006). Unlike individual counseling, not every group member will be able to discuss his or her own concerns in depth; group work provides a place for members to listen and learn from one another, and think about what has been talked about (Wagner & Ingersoll, in press).

The VCS presents another avenue for clients to discuss the target behavior, particularly when there is ambivalence. Our earlier DUI client in the first part of this chapter is Client 5 in the group example. He was relatively quiet throughout the group until he stated that he had picked "stability" as a value and how this really surprised him. He learned something new about himself. When the discussion centered on how alcohol had impacted values, he began to examine himself and his drinking in a new light. He was much more open to looking at the role of drinking in his life as this insight came from him—in other words, he wasn't told this by his social worker. He ended his conversation with need for change talk: "Maybe I should do something about my drinking." A follow-up group might cover strategies to quit or reduce drinking, which would be something he would be much more open to, after this exercise.

FINAL THOUGHTS

Ambivalence can wax and wane (Miller & Rollnick, 2002). We can all think of times when we were more motivated to do something and then we weren't. Like in the example of my father-in-law, when something becomes important enough for us, we can move forward if we have the confidence to do it. Focusing on change talk in client conversations can help tip the balance in favor of change. Research has demonstrated its importance and the role that practitioners play in shaping the language that our clients use. Utilizing MI skills and structured exercises can be helpful in this endeavor.

7

Rolling with Resistance

Motivational Interviewing with Adolescents, or "You Can't Make Me"

WITH ELIZABETH BARNETT
AND AUDREY M. SHILLINGTON

Social workers are accustomed to working with clients who aren't always happy to be receiving their services. MI trainers occasionally have classes with trainees who were "made" to attend by their employers, and some promptly show their thoughts about the whole thing by pulling out the newspaper to read or checking their mobile phones during the training. I (MH) once had an undergraduate student who was a business major told to take my human behavior class because he "needed to learn how to get along with people." What all of these people have in common is a loss of their autonomy: they are forced to do something by someone else or, as may be the case with some clients, by conditions beyond their control. As we learned in self-determination theory, humans have a need for autonomy. In social work lingo, clients need to have self-determination. Reactance theory tells us that when autonomy or self-determination is threatened, humans will react or "push back" to assert their autonomy (Brehm & Brehm, 1981). This "push-back" is termed resistance in MI.

Miller and Rollnick (1999) frame resistance a bit differently from what we were taught in social work school. Classic definitions of resistance were from the psychodynamic perspective, in that resistance is something that resides within the client and serves as an obstacle to personal growth or change (Hepworth et al., 2010). The task of the therapist is to overcome this obstacle through interpretation or, as in the case of traditional substance use treatment, through confronting a client about their "denial" (Glabbard, Beck, & Holmes, 2005). In this perspective, people experience resistance because it is painful to examine oneself. Thus clients respond by trying to cover up their repressed thoughts or the insights that are provided in the therapy process. Resistance is seen as a *client* problem; this viewpoint is evident when we hear social work students still discuss "transference" issues that their clients experience. When clients respond to them by being argumentative or passive, students sometimes view this reaction as due to something internal that a client is experiencing. The behaviors that they are seeing are viewed very differently through an MI lens.

Taking a more client-centered view, Miller and Rollnick (2002, p. 98) describe resistance as "an observable client behavior" that "represents an important signal of dissonance within the counseling process." Resistance or denial is not a trait within the client but is a *response* to the interpersonal communication between clients and their social workers. When resistant behaviors are observed, it is our job as social workers to stop, reflect on what just happened in the interaction, and proceed to communicate in a different manner. This is called *rolling with resistance,* and strategies for "rolling" are described below.

As research progressed in the area of understanding client speech within MI interviews, it became apparent that some distinction needed to be made regarding what Miller and Rollnick (1999) had previously indicated was resistance. The term *sustain talk* was adopted to better differentiate client speech regarding maintaining the status quo from behaviors that could indicate resistance. It is normal for clients to discuss their concerns about change, and there was concern that calling this type of speech "resistance" might pathologize this type of communication (Miller, Moyers, Amrhein, & Rollnick, 2006). Resistance is signaled by behaviors that clients use to indicate dissonance in the interaction. Such behaviors include arguing or interrupting; changing the subject; and discounting or disagreeing with what the social worker is saying. Other clients can refuse to talk at all, or they may take over the whole conversation (Rosengren, 2009).

What can cause a client to become resistant? Sometimes the context of the interaction can create clients who want to resist from the get-go. Trainees who are mandated to a workshop can come in deciding that the training will be a waste of time and they will only be taught what they know and do already anyway, or this whole MI thing is just another flavor of the month. Mandated clients may approach their social worker with distrust and with their guard up, ready to argue with everything the social worker has to say in order to protect their families. Racial, ethnic, age, or class differences can put minority clients in a wary frame of mind in an interview (Woller, Buboltz, & Loveland, 2007). Clients with serious mental illness may worry that they will be judged or made to take medications. Adolescents who are working through normal developmental issues around autonomy may be highly suspicious of anything an adult in authority has to say (Naar-King & Suarez, 2011). All of these situations present us with resistant trainees/clients who are meeting us with *normal* responses to having their autonomy threatened. It is how we respond to this resistance that sets the stage for future interactions.

I (MH) recently was sharing a story with a friend who is an elementary school teacher. I told her about a trainee who had given me a hard time in a workshop. She asked me, "Couldn't you just tell him that if he didn't like it, he could leave? That's what I do: I send kids who misbehave to the principal's office." I explained to her how doing that would defeat what I was trying to model in training MI! Unfortunately, many of us meet resistance with resistance head on by using our "default" methods of communication. Other times, we inadvertently stumble right into communication traps such as arguing or labeling (Gaume, Bertholet, Faouzi, Gmel, & Daeppen, 2010).

Miller and Rollnick (1999) discuss "communication traps" that can block communication and in worst cases, create or increase client resistance. We already discussed in Chapter 3 the *question–answer trap* whereby we ask our clients question after question. Clients in return may not become overtly resistant but may go in the other direction of being overtly passive and just give us minimal information and never quite engage in the conversation. The *blaming trap* would be the one described in the story above: if trainees/clients aren't engaged, then it is their problem. When I (MH) worked in substance use treatment, "resistant" clients would be discharged from residential treatment as they "needed to go out to hit bottom" before they could be motivated. The blame for the lack of motivation, or remaining in "denial," rested squarely on them. We only took the responsibility when our clients did well!

A number of things that social work professionals do with clients who show resistant behaviors can actually be counterproductive (Forrester et al., 2008). The *expert trap* is a version of the *righting reflex*. We want to tell our clients what to do and what is in their best interests. We have lots of ideas about how they can fix their lives. When they discount these ideas, or tell us why they won't work, we are surprised. We can fall into the *shaming trap* of, "I was just trying to help." This can be a version of the *labeling trap*, whereby we can stick a label on the client or behavior, such as "resistant" or "in denial" or "drug addict" or "uncaring mother." Warnings or threats may appear, whereby if we can't convince clients to make the particular change, we can tell them what will happen if they don't make the change. We can use the *taking sides trap* by arguing for change or by agreeing with some other party who might be involved. An example of this would be, "Can't you see that your parents are worried about you and only want what is in your best interest?" Finally, the *premature focus trap* is where we move ahead of clients, usually to the change process, without fully exploring their ambivalence. Clients may balk at the discussion and utilize a great deal of sustain talk to explain why they can't, won't, shouldn't, make the change.

To summarize, clients may come to us ready to engage in sustain talk or with resistant behaviors based on the context of the interview. We can fall into communication traps that serve as ways for us to try to stay in control of the conversation, and usually these methods fail. Whenever we hear a great deal of sustain talk or observe resistant behaviors, our clients are signaling to us that we are not communicating well with them—that whatever we are doing is threatening their autonomy and they are "pushing back."

ROLLING WITH RESISTANCE STRATEGIES

MI trainers love a good mnemonic device, and a clever trainer came up with ways to remember the rolling with resistance strategies as SAD and SCARED. We don't know if clients who are being resistant are really sad or scared, but this idea helps us remember to think about what they are presently going through. SAD stands for *simple reflections, amplified reflections,* and *double-sided reflections.* Let's take a look at these methods for rolling with resistance first.

Resistance in an interaction can feel like a large sailboat that is moving in a particular direction, very quickly. The boat is gathering momentum as it moves, and as the social worker in the interview, we may feel that the conversation is definitely going off-course, particularly if we have an angry client who is more interested in telling us off than in discussing the concern at hand. *Simple reflections* allow us to not get drawn into arguments and at the same time they let clients know that we are listening to them. A reflection takes the "wind out of the sails" so to speak, and the boat becomes dead in the water—the energy to keep this kind of communication going seems to dissipate. John Martin, an MI trainer, often says, "When in doubt, reflect." Reflecting stops the negative flow of energy and also gives us time to gather our thoughts and think about how to best handle the resistance we are seeing.

Using *simple reflections* helps us understand what clients are trying to say while we are simultaneously trying to decide where the resistance might be coming from. Perhaps we inadvertently came off as being an expert or created a premature focus by bringing up a particular topic or linking topics together before a client was ready to make that leap. Resistance can also come from the context, and using simple reflections signals to clients that we aren't going to judge them or argue our point, but track along with them. *Amplified reflections* are where we overstate what we hear clients saying, which sometimes allows them to reduce their "push-back." Some examples of amplified reflections are given in the following dialogue between an adolescent client and a school social worker:

CLIENT: Why should I talk to you … you have no idea what my life is like!

SOCIAL WORKER: It's impossible for anyone to really get what you are going through [amplified reflection].

CLIENT: Well, it's not as bad as that; I have friends …

SOCIAL WORKER: You find it really helpful to talk to your friends [amplified reflection].

CLIENT: Well, we don't really talk, but I don't want to be discussing my problems with some social worker.

SOCIAL WORKER: So on the one hand, you're kind of dealing with stuff by yourself, and on the other hand, it might be nice to have someone to discuss what is going on with you as long as you could trust that person [double-sided reflection].

Double-sided reflections are those that reflect clients' ambivalence that sometimes they can be unaware of. Using double-sided reflections helps link both sides of the ambivalence, and as we discussed in Chapter 7, this helps to develop discrepancy. Placing what you want your clients to remember in the last part of the reflection helps to maintain the direction of your conversation as well. In the above dialogue, the social worker placed the last emphasis on the client's desire to not be so isolated with the problem she is dealing with.

The SCARED mnemonic stands for *shifting focus, coming alongside, agreement with a twist, reframing, emphasizing personal control,* and *disclosing feelings.* The *shifting focus* method is about changing the subject or steering the conversation in a different direction. In the preceding example, for instance, the social worker could ask, "What do you look for in people whom you trust?" This takes the conversation away from the client's argument that the social worker can't understand her. We can also shift focus in a more obvious manner, but it is done in a way that is respectful of clients: "We don't seem to be getting to an agreement here. I am wondering if it would be OK to move on to another topic?"

Coming alongside is a strategy used to side with clients' perspectives, particularly when we hear a lot of sustain talk as to why they can't change, or this isn't the time to change. My (MH) favorite example of this comes from a role play I did with an MSW graduate student when I was a guest speaker in a class, presenting on MI. She told me her issue was that she was a "slob." As we discussed her sloppiness, she proceeded to tell me why it was a problem and then all the reasons why she couldn't change. I told her, "Perhaps now is not the time to change this; you have so much else on your plate as a graduate student, this is the last thing you need to worry about." The student looked at me like I was crazy and then began to discuss all the ways she could make the change. Coming alongside does not always work this dramatically, but it definitely changes the momentum of the conversation. Miller and Rollnick (2002) indicate that it is important to gauge the use of this method by making sure it decreases resistance and/or sustain talk, and elicits change talk; if clients continue in sustain talk, then perhaps a different strategy might be better.

Agreement with a twist is an agreement or a reflection (simple or complex) that has a reframe tacked on to it (the twist) (Miller & Rollnick, 2002; Rosengren, 2009). This helps us to align with clients but to move the conversation in a different direction. In continuing the conversation with the adolescent from above, the social worker might reply, "You are careful about who you talk to and you know that when you need to, you have found it helpful to open up to people who you trust." The first part is the agreement (reflection) and the second is the twist: the client didn't say this but it was implied. The twist moves the conversation into the direction of how the client found it helpful to talk to people in the past.

Reframing is a method for rolling with resistance that is familiar to social workers. It involves taking something clients have said and "framing" it in a different way, so that clients have a different perspective or way to look at a situation (Miller & Rollnick, 2002). A reframe of the client's statement that she is distrustful of the social worker could be, "Not trusting strangers until you get to know them is a logical way to protect one-self." This casts the behavior as "normal" with the underlying message that once she gets to know the worker, she may be more trusting.

If clients become resistant when they feel their autonomy being threatened, then it is evident why *emphasizing personal control* can be an effective strategy to roll with resistance. "Only you can make the decision about when you can trust someone" or "The decision to change is entirely up to you; only you can make that choice" are two examples of how we can acknowledge to clients that change is truly up to them. Even in mandated settings, clients still ultimately have choices (Miller & Rollnick, 2002).

Disclosing personal feelings is a strategy that is not used too often but can be useful in the right circumstances. It can be an acknowledgment of falling into a communication trap: "I'm sorry if I was getting ahead of you and this got you upset. Let's back up, if that is OK with you." It can also be used when clients make decisions that put themselves at risk: "I am very concerned that you are practicing unsafe sex." Typically we do not share our feelings with clients, but sometimes the moment might be right for this to occur (Rosengren, 2009).

MI AND ADOLESCENTS

Rolling with resistance skills are often needed in social work with adolescents who by nature are challenging and questioning of those in authority. Conclusions about the appropriateness of MI with adolescents are generated from its ability to produce effects in many of the existing research studies. These conclusions are based on Blos's (1966) theory of development, which categorizes adolescence as a time of separation and individuation, when making choices for oneself is paramount. More evidence for its use with adolescents is taken from studies showing that MI is most effective with those who are least motivated to change (Brown & Lourie, 2001; Miller & Rose, 2009), as well as successful in reaching nontreatment-seeking participants (Miller & Sovereign, 1989). Since adolescents are often mandated to attend counseling or treatment by doctors, school officials, juvenile justice professionals, or families, they often fall into these categories of nontreatment seeking and not motivated for change. Adolescence is also known as a time when reactance is at its height (Hong, Giannakopoulos, Laing, & Williams, 1994); thus a nonconfrontational approach is imperative to achieve success with this population (Hohman & Kleinpeter, 2009; Naar-King & Suarez, 2011).

MI interventions with adolescents have focused on:

- Sexual risk behaviors (Brown & Lourie, 2001; Cowley, Farley, & Beamis, 2002; Naar-King et al., 2006)
- Alcohol problems (Miller, Turner, & Marlatt, 2001; Monti, Colby, & O'Leary, 2001)
- Drug use (Baer et al., 2007; Martin & Copeland, 2008; McCambridge, Slym, & Strang, 2008; Peterson, Baer, Wells, Ginzler, & Garrett, 2006; Stephens et al., 2004; Swan et al., 2008; Walker, Roffman, Stephens-Wakana, & Berghuis, 2006; Winters & Leitten, 2007; Winters, Leitten, Wagner, & Tevyaw, 2007)
- Tobacco use (Colby et al., 1998, 2005; Helstrom, Hutchison, & Bryan, 2007; Kelly & Lapworth, 2006; Vaughan, Levy, & Knight, 2003; Woodruff, Edwards, Conway, & Elliott, 2001)
- Eating disorders (Dunn, Neighbors, & Larimer, 2006)
- Depression (Brody, 2009)
- School attendance (Atkinson & Woods, 2003; Enea & Dafinoiu, 2009; Rutschman, 2010)

School settings have also been successfully utilized for motivational interviews for both alcohol and drug use (Kaplan, Engle, Austin, & Wagner, 2011). Winters and Leitten (2007) found that students identified as drug users who receive a motivational interview, either alone or with a parent, improved in number of days of using illicit drugs, drinking and binge drinking, as well as drug-related consequences, relative to the assessment-only control group. These improvements were found at the 6-month follow-up. Grenard and colleagues (2007) used MI in alternative high schools for substance use. The study revealed that students were willing to discuss their drug use and that the intervention impacted their readiness to change their drug use. Another high school based study was focused on using MI to reduce school truancy. The investigators found a 61% reduction in truancy rates in the treatment group (Enea & Dafinoiu, 2009).

MOTIVATIONAL INTERVIEWING WITH ADOLESCENTS: EXAMPLE AND DIALOGUE

High school dropout is a major problem in the United States, with over a million students a year quitting high school before graduation; a majority of these are minority students (Nowicki, Duke, Sisney, Strickler, & Tyler,

2004). Costs of high school dropout includes direct costs to the student in terms of lost wages over time, medical costs for uninsured health care, and crime-related costs, among others (Alliance for Excellent Education, 2008). The following case example demonstrates an MI interview for school non-attendance.

Robert Martinez is a school social worker who works in a community that is economically in transition. His school district is concerned with a rise in their high school dropout rate over the past few years. Given this concern, Mr. Martinez has been asked to run a pilot program to provide MI interventions with students who have missed more than 5 days in the school year that were not due to excused illness. The hope is that intervening with these students early before they miss more school may impact their decision to drop out in the future. Students who have excessive absences or other risks for dropout are referred to meet with him by their teachers or counselors. Mr. Martinez uses MI with the goal of reengaging students in school.

Shawn is a 15-year-old African American male who is in the 10th grade. He has missed 5 days of school and his teachers report that when he is in school, he does not appear interested in class. He frequently forgets his homework, but his grades are mainly B's and C's since he does well on tests. Shawn has been in trouble for sleeping in class on three occasions. He is told by the vice principal that he must meet with Mr. Martinez before he can return to school since he has missed 5 days of school.

Once again, we will be coding the dialogue using the following codes as well as noting rolling with resistance strategies:

• GI = giving information	• MIA = MI adherent
• SR = simple reflection	(affirming, asking permission,
• CR = complex reflection	emphasizing personal control,
• OQ = open-ended question	support)
• CQ = closed-ended question	

SOCIAL WORKER: Hi, Shawn. My name is Mr. Martinez and I am a social worker with the school.

CLIENT: Yeah, I was told that I had to come talk to you before I could go back to school.

SOCIAL WORKER: Not exactly what you had in mind when you came to school today, to have to go talk to a stranger [CR].

CLIENT: Yeah, this is stupid. Like what are you going to tell me that I don't already know?

SOCIAL WORKER: This might be a real waste of your time [CR—amplified reflection].

CLIENT: Whatever.

SOCIAL WORKER: You are thinking that I am going to lecture you about attending school [CR—coming alongside].

CLIENT: Sure, that's your job, right?

SOCIAL WORKER: Only you can make the decision about what is right for you regarding school [MIA—emphasizing personal control].

CLIENT: You got that right. Adults are always trying to make me do stuff, and I just blow them off.

SOCIAL WORKER: People don't seem to understand that you are able to make good decisions about what is right for you [CR—agreement with a twist].

CLIENT: Yeah, I know how to take care of myself—and other people too.

SOCIAL WORKER: How do you take care of yourself [OQ—shifting focus]?

CLIENT: I do OK. Maybe school isn't my thing, but I am good at other stuff. I make sure to make something to eat for me and my little brother when my mom has to work late. My friends know that they can trust me, that I have their backs.

SOCIAL WORKER: Taking care of your brother and your friends are things that you do well, too [SR].

CLIENT: Yeah.

SOCIAL WORKER: What other things do you do well [OQ]?

CLIENT: I dunno. My mom would say I'm a good kid except she gets on my case when I miss school.

SOCIAL WORKER: School is important to her [CR].

CLIENT: Yeah but she's not the one who has be here. It's so lame! The teachers just get on you all the time, tell you to do this, do that.

SOCIAL WORKER: So sometimes school is a pain because the work is boring or the teachers ask for too much [SR]. What else don't you like about school [OQ]?

CLIENT: Well, it's just boring. I'd much rather be at home watching TV or playing video games.

SOCIAL WORKER: It's not as interesting as other things you could be doing [SR].

CLIENT: I stay up late too, playing video games or being on the computer, so who wants to get up in the morning? And once I am late, I figure I might as well just stay home. Wouldn't you?

SOCIAL WORKER: The day seems like it is already blown once you are late. Might as well just take the absence instead of a tardy [CR].

CLIENT: Yeah, you get it.

SOCIAL WORKER: If I could ask you this, Shawn [MIA—asking for permission]: as you look down the road, say to the end of this year, what will things be like for you if you miss more school [OQ]?

CLIENT: I dunno.

SOCIAL WORKER: It's hard to know or even guess what might happen [SR— coming alongside].

CLIENT: Well, I guess I might have to do 10th grade over again. I mean, my grades are still OK. I could probably pass with D's 'cause I am smart, ya know? So I might not have to repeat. But if I did, I guess I would just quit. I'd be 16 and I could go get a job. My mom could use the money.

SOCIAL WORKER: So getting a job full-time might be helpful to your mom, and on the other hand, she wouldn't be really happy about you quitting since she thinks school is important [CR—double-sided reflection].

CLIENT: No, she would be mad. But like I said, she's not the one who has to be here.

SOCIAL WORKER: If you look down the road, and say you were to drop out, what might be the downside of doing that [OQ—eliciting reason change talk]?

CLIENT: I dunno. Maybe it would be hard to get a job. And my friends would still be in school so I could play video games by myself all day but that might get boring too.

SOCIAL WORKER: What else [OQ]?

CLIENT: People might think I did it 'cause I was stupid, which would be *wrong*. I am really smart.

SOCIAL WORKER: People might misinterpret why you quit or say things about you [CR].

CLIENT: Yeah.

SOCIAL WORKER: So if you were to keep coming to school, what might be the pay-off for you [OQ—eliciting reason change talk]?

CLIENT: I'd be with my friends. I could show people that I was smart, wanted to make something out of my life. I want to get a really good job, not some stupid one like I could get if I quit. My mom wants me to go to college. But who knows about that.

SOCIAL WORKER: You want people to look up to you and understand that you are smart—which I know is true, your teachers have told me—and you'd be with your friends, and having a high school diploma would help you get a better job [SR; MIA—affirming]. Right now, Shawn, how motivated are you to stay in school, say, on a scale of 1, not motivated, to 10, motivated [OQ—change ruler]?

CLIENT: (*Shrugs.*) I guess I am a 6.

SOCIAL WORKER: Wow—that is high [MIA—support]. Why are you a 6 and not a, say, 4 [OQ]?

CLIENT: I *know* I have to come to school. I don't want to be like those guys I see just hanging out on the street, nothing to do, looking bored, just being with each other. It's just that I am bored here too. But I know I can't be staying home, missing school much more.

SOCIAL WORKER: Why is that [OQ]?

CLIENT: Well, I know that if I miss more school, then my mom will get a letter and will have to go to a hearing.

SOCIAL WORKER: Yes, that's true [GI]. So what is your goal? What will you do [OQ—key question]?

CLIENT: I will keep coming to school.

SOCIAL WORKER: You won't be missing any more days unless you're sick [CR]. What do you need to help you keep this commitment [OQ]?

CLIENT: Maybe you could talk to my teachers and maybe get some of them to not be so mean. Or maybe I could come talk to you sometimes?

SOCIAL WORKER: Yes, I am always happy to talk to you. But I don't know if I can change your teachers [GI]. What could you do when you talk to them [OQ]?

CLIENT: I dunno. Maybe I could at least try to, you know, like not sleep in class. Turn in my homework even though I think it's stupid.

SOCIAL WORKER: Making an effort on your end might help show them you mean business [CR]. What other things can you do to make this a little easier on yourself [OQ]?

CLIENT: Maybe I could tell my mom to wake me up in the morning. She works late and likes to sleep in herself. I stay up waiting for her. We're both tired in the morning. But maybe she would help me out.

SOCIAL WORKER: What else might help make coming to school easier on yourself [OQ]?

CLIENT: Well, if I didn't have to pick my little brother up after school, then maybe I could be in a sport, like basketball. But my mom expects me to do this. Maybe I could get my next door neighbor to get him for a few hours. I'd have to ask my mom. I've always wanted to play, and my friends tell me that I could make the team, easy.

SOCIAL WORKER: So let me see if I got everything that will help you with your plan to come to school every day: You will talk to your mom to see if she will get you up on time, so you won't be late and tempted to just say the heck with it; you are going to make an effort to turn in your homework and at least try to pretend that you like some of your teachers; and you are going to see about getting some help with your little brother so that you can try out for the basketball team. You might want to even come back and check in with me from time to time [SR].

CLIENT: Yeah, that's about right. I can do that stuff.

SOCIAL WORKER: Sounds like you are responsible, like in how you take care of your brother, and when you put your mind to do something, you do it [MIA—affirming]. Can I ask, how confident are you that you can do all these things [OQ]?

CLIENT: Very confident. You are right, I always do what I say. Don't worry, Mr. Martinez. I'll keep coming.

SOCIAL WORKER: Glad to hear it. Please come by anytime you want.

DISCUSSION

This interview was used for demonstration purposes and would not be an entire interview. It also presented a student who was at moderate risk for school dropout. A motivational interview with an older, higher-risk student who was ready to drop out may have gone in a different direction, and the social worker's goal may have been to help strategize plans for the future, if the youth was not willing to stay in school.

Mr. Martinez had to roll with Shawn's resistance from the very beginning of the interview. He used several different strategies, including amplified reflections, coming alongside, and emphasizing personal control. This allowed Shawn to begin to engage with him, and Shawn himself brought up the topic of missing school. He was then open to discussing the future should he keep missing school or decide to attend school. The social worker used a change ruler to elicit reason change talk about why continued school attendance is important to Shawn. After reflecting Shawn's comments, Mr. Martinez then asked a *key question*—"What will you do?"—as a way to secure commitment from Shawn. Key questions are asked when the practitioner senses that the client is ready to move forward (Miller & Rollnick, 2002; Rosengren, 2009) and is a way to guide the conversation in the direction of change.

In *developing a plan*, another aspect of an MI interview, Mr. Martinez asked Shawn to describe barriers to school attendance and formulate his own strategies for overcoming them. He then pulled all the content of the interview together in a summary. Finally, Shawn was asked how confident he was that he could do all of these behaviors, which was a way for Mr. Martinez to ask for a commitment (commitment change talk) from him to the plan.

Some of you reading this might say, "Wait a minute—this kid looks depressed. Shouldn't the social worker be asking him about that?" Shawn presents with some of the risk factors for school dropout, which included (1) a mother whose job demands make it difficult for her to focus on her children's schooling and (2) attending to his younger brother's needs from school pick-up to bedtime. Shawn also has support for school attendance through his peers. He doesn't miss school to spend time with his own friends or older adults but to be alone at home with his video games. He misses class due to sleeping in, and he often does not turn in his homework. Depression? Perhaps. The focus of this interview was his school truancy. Sometimes when using MI we are tempted to stray from the target behavior and we lose our direction. Of course, this is necessary when clients begin to discuss suicidal ideation or are recipients of physical abuse. For this particular interview, the social worker kept his focus on school attendance but mentally made notes of the reasons for Shawn's truancy. He could choose to follow up this interview with a second one to screen Shawn for depression.

FINAL THOUGHTS

Clients, particularly adolescents, may come to us already resistant due to the nature of the situation or setting where they are being interviewed.

Pressuring or arguing for change can increase resistance even more. Rolling with resistance strategies allow us to deflect the resistance and at the same time allow clients to know that they have been heard. We are not going to push them to change but will instead help guide them to resolve their ambivalence about change. Rolling with resistance keeps us in the spirit of MI as we seek to keep a collaborative tone that encourages client autonomy.

8

Building Collaboration

Motivational Interviewing
in Community Organization Work

WITH MIKE EICHLER

MaryAnn is a 28-year-old recent graduate of an MSW program who has always been interested in community organizing. Recently she interviewed for a position with this focus at a community-based agency. To her delight, she was hired. The agency she is a part of is considering building a teenage alcohol use prevention coalition of parents, local youth, school groups, teen recreation center leaders, religious leaders, the police, community leaders, and local business people. One of MaryAnn's first goals is to meet with these various stakeholders individually, to determine if there is even interest or concern in the community regarding teenage alcohol use and if so, whether her agency could be a resource in addressing this problem. MaryAnn is in charge of working with business leaders and community leaders. She knows that research has shown that environmental responses in the prevention area have produced good results. Some of these include increasing identification checks at alcohol sales points and increasing legal penalties for those who do not ask for identification or sell to minors. MaryAnn studied MI in graduate school and wants to apply some of the principles and skills of individual work in MI to help her as she works to listen and motivate individuals to come on board. She plans to use MI to facilitate the collaboration of these individuals with each other once she brings them together as a group. She thinks her task should be pretty easy; who isn't interested in reducing teenage alcohol use?

Macro interventions typically target the environment, policies, and/or prevailing norms to address social problems (Kirst-Ashman & Hull, 2009). Applying MI to community organizing (CO) work and other forms of macro interventions is still an emerging field. Two studies have used MI as part of the process to develop alcohol prevention programs on university campuses (Miller, Toscava, Miller, & Sanchez, 2000; Newbery, McCambridge, & Strang, 2007), but did not describe how MI facilitated the organizing process. While it is beyond the scope of this chapter to present detailed information regarding the types and methods of macro social work, we will provide some background on CO work in order to consider how MI is applied in that context.

CO strategies have been built on organizing around the power of confrontation from a group to challenge the power of those with influence. Built on a model developed by Saul Alinsky (1971), community organizing in the past has involved taking a group with an issue—unemployment, poor housing, environmental problems—and organizing them to picket, protest, publicly embarrass, or demonstrate against those who have the power to fix the problem (Kirst-Ashman & Hull, 2009). The organizer's job is to bring together people, typically called stakeholders, who feel strongly about an issue, tie this issue to their self-interest, and coach them on methods of organizing for change. This may mean the formation of a coalition of various community members to obtain an outcome that is in their common interest. Pressure is exerted through the methods described above in order to force change. This model has been called conflict organizing.

There are other models that are less confrontational. For instance, President Obama worked as a community organizer in Chicago's South Side where his methods still involved making demands for change from those in power (York, 2008). He utilized individual interviews to determine people's self-interests and worked with community members to develop leadership from within. In this case, his organizing led to the establishment of a youth employment office in a low-income housing project and to the removal of asbestos from the housing (Obama, 2007).

An application of MI to CO involves thinking about of the type of CO model the social worker or agency wants to use and determining if this model is congruent with the spirit of MI. We know that demanding, embarrassing, or confronting the individual clients we work with may lead to some sort of compliance that is only motivated by external forces but will not lead to lasting change. And, as we learned with reactance theory, individuals often "push back" and argue against change in order to maintain their autonomy. The same is true when the social worker is working with community leaders, housing administrators, or banking executives: creating real change comes from engaging them and learning what is important, what they value, and what they need. Working from a collaborative position is more likely to lead to internally motivated change that benefits all parties (Eichler, 2007).

MI AND CONSENSUS ORGANIZING

One CO method that is a good fit with MI is that of consensus organizing (Eichler, 2007). Consensus organizing is radically different from Alinsky's conflict model in that the focus is on bringing together both community members and members of the power structure to address a problem. While similar to the model that President Obama used, consensus organizing goes beyond that by utilizing client-centered theory as one of its foundations. Community organizers who use consensus organizing recognize the potential for positive support from the various stakeholders who might become involved. The CO worker is optimistic about people's abilities to create change, whether they are from poor, depressed communities or are leaders who hold power. Goals and strategies are determined by the coalition of stakeholders, not the CO worker or agency. The overarching approach is that everyone in the group is valued and respected (Eichler, 2007).

The process of consensus organizing begins by building relationships on the individual level, learning of the individual's self-interests and goals regarding the problem under discussion, and then bringing interested individuals together as a group to articulate their concerns and strategize methods to address them. The role of the CO worker is to engage individual stakeholders, provide hope and optimism, find commonalities among them, and assist them in a group process to develop their own strategies for change. Relationships are based on respect and mutual benefit. Interconnections between stakeholders are highlighted, and each individual is seen as indispensable to the process (Eichler, 2007).

As shown on Table 8.1, utilizing the skills of MI can help implement the consensus organizing model. Utilizing the principles of MI can provide a framework for the integration of these two models. In the initial stages, the CO worker meets with individual stakeholders. As discussed earlier in this book, we engage and build collaboration with clients by using MI OARS skills (express empathy). MI conversations always begin with curiosity, with the social worker or CO worker wanting to learn from the stakeholders. Stakeholders are asked for their thoughts, ideas, values, and motivators. Using their responses, the social worker/community organizer enters their world, culture, and context, to understand their viewpoints of the situation under discussion. Those new to CO in particular aren't always used to interviewing store owners, bank administrators, or business executives, and it is helpful to suspend preconceptions to truly learn what is important to interviewees (Eichler, 2007).

Supporting the stakeholder's autonomy is another way to build collaboration and trust as stakeholders or clients recognize that the social worker isn't going to judge them, tell them what to do, or force them into some kind of role. Collaboration also involves understanding their aspirations (what they want from the situation), and the social worker may convey his or her own aspirations for the client or community (Miller & Rollnick, 2002). If the stakeholder makes a decision that is not congruent with what the community organizer is trying to achieve, the social worker/community organizer does not attempt to argue or persuade the client to do otherwise. Acceptance of stakeholders' decisions, even when it is something the social worker doesn't agree with, may eventually further possible collaboration in the future. Stakeholders may not believe that the proposed change is good for them personally, even if they acknowledge that it may benefit others. If that is the case, then it is important to find what is important to the individual stakeholder and what might be of benefit to him or her. As Miller and Rollnick (2002) state, we "cannot use MI to induce behavior change unless the client perceives that such change ... is in his or her own best interest." (p. 167).

Stakeholders may tell the CO worker that they don't have the time, aren't interested, or think that working with a developing coalition may be detrimental to their own purposes. In consensus organizing, this is conceptualized as resistance; in MI this would be viewed as sustain talk and the CO worker could use roll with resistance strategies, such as the use of reflections, reframing, coming alongside, and/or emphasizing choice and personal control (see Chapter 7 for more on these methods). Double-sided reflections help to develop discrepancy between what the stakeholder

TABLE 8.1. Comparison of Consensus Organizing Strategies and MI Principles and Skills

Consensus organizing strategies	MI principles/skills
Engage individuals	Express empathy; OARS skills
Learn of self-interest/motivators, similar values/goals; concerns	OARS; develop discrepancy
Disinterest seen as resistance	Roll with resistance strategies
Not everyone will be interested	Support autonomy to refuse to participate
Ask to join stakeholders	Secure commitment
Problem is defined by community/ stakeholders	Agenda setting; support autonomy
Learn group members' common concerns and goals	OARS; DARN change talk
Design own strategies as a group	OARS skills
Designed by partners, not professionals	Support autonomy
Specific roles based on unique skills	Support autonomy; affirmations
Secure commitment	Secure commitment
Find new partners as needed	Collaboration
Provide support and encouragement	Express hope and optimism
Appreciate individuals in the process	Affirmations

thinks might happen and his or her values, for instance. If an individual stakeholder has no concern or ambivalence about the problem under discussion, then the CO worker supports his or her autonomy by not arguing or pressuring him or her. If the stakeholder is interested, then the CO worker secures commitment to attend a larger group meeting.

CONSENSUS ORGANIZING: EXAMPLE AND DIALOGUE

MaryAnn has studied consensus organizing as well as MI and knows that her first step is to find out the concerns regarding the problem and the corresponding self-interests of the stakeholders she is assigned to meet. Community members, including clergy, parents, police, and school administrators, so far have been very supportive, with some of them calling for changes in the local laws to reduce underage alcohol access. This whole movement started following the deaths of three local teenagers in the past year due to drinking and driving. She is warned that local liquor store and convenience store owners and operators might not be so supportive, especially if they are hearing talk of increased requirements and legal sanctions. MaryAnn is curious as to what their self-interests might be and uses OARS skills to learn about their situations as well as to begin to develop collaboration. She meets with one owner of a liquor store, to determine if he has concerns and if so, to invite him to join their developing coalition. She listens closely to determine what his motivators and values are (see underlined text):

Once again, we will code the interactions using the following:

- GI = giving information
- SR = simple reflection
- CR = complex reflection
- OQ = open-ended question
- CQ = closed-ended question

- MIA = MI adherent (affirming, asking permission, emphasizing personal control, support)

SOCIAL WORKER: Hi, Mr. Kamdar. My name is MaryAnn Wheeler and I am with the Community Solutions agency. Thank you for taking the time to meet with me today. If it would be OK with you, I wanted to discuss some thoughts that have come up in the community regarding a possible teen alcohol prevention initiative [MIA]. I am very interested in your perspective, as a community member and a store owner [GI].

STAKEHOLDER: Sure, I have a few minutes until I have to get back to work.

SOCIAL WORKER: As you know, we had three teen drunk driving deaths this past year, and some community members have indicated that they would like to see some things change so that we can avoid more deaths like that in the future. I am trying to understand what other community members think and learn if teen alcohol use, and drinking and driving, are concerns to them. I am also trying to determine if my agency can be a resource on this for community members [GI].

STAKEHOLDER: Yes, yes, that whole thing with the car accident was terrible. Of course, I felt just awful when I heard about it. But it wasn't my fault. It's not like I sold alcohol to those kids or sell it to any other teenagers. What would you want from me?

SOCIAL WORKER: You're wondering what your role would be since you make sure your store is in compliance with state regulations [CR].

STAKEHOLDER: Yeah, I follow all those rules. Of course, I can't always control my employees, especially when I am not here. <u>I get worried</u> that one of those decoys the cops send is going to come in here when I'm not around and my employee will forget to card him [ask for identification] and then we're busted. But I tell them all the time to make sure that they card everyone who looks under 30.

SOCIAL WORKER: So on the one hand, you really make an effort to follow the state and local laws, and on the other, you are concerned that one of these days a decoy will come in and your employee will make a mistake [CR—developing discrepancy].

STAKEHOLDER: Those decoys look older than 21 so it is easy to screw up! I have heard talk about making even stricter laws and requirements around alcohol sales. <u>I don't need</u> a bunch of cops and other people sitting around making up more rules that will make it harder for me to run my business.

SOCIAL WORKER: You are thinking that other people in our community might make some new laws that could affect your business negatively without any input from you [CR—coming alongside].

STAKEHOLDER: Well, I hear things. What can I do? <u>I don't want teenagers to drink or drink and drive</u>, but <u>I don't want other people telling me how to run my business</u>. They think it is the storeowner's fault when kids get alcohol. I don't sell to them, I check licenses, and I watch for theft. But sometimes it just happens. Lots of kids just get alcohol from their own homes!

SOCIAL WORKER: You feel singled out as a store owner when you know the problem has many sources [CR]. One of the things my agency can do is help organize a meeting, for many different people to get together and figure out common concerns and then some common strategies. Teenage alcohol use is a complex problem, and there are many different reasons teens drink and just as many ways to prevent this. It is not just one group's—like storeowners—problem [GI]. What would your interest be in attending such a meeting [OQ]?

STAKEHOLDER: Well, maybe I would come. That way I could make sure no one would be passing new laws without my input.

SOCIAL WORKER: If you were to come, what do you think some of the other advantages would be, to you as a business owner [OQ—supporting autonomy; eliciting reason change talk]?

STAKEHOLDER: Well, <u>I want people to think that I do care </u>about what goes on in this community … my son was friends with one of those boys who was killed. <u>I don't want him or any of his friends to get involved with alcohol</u>. But I don't want to go to some meeting where people are putting down people like me! It's hard to turn a profit and <u>I don't want things to get harder</u>.

SOCIAL WORKER: You are concerned that a group could make decisions that could adversely affect you, and you are also concerned about what happens to kids in this community [CR]. You are caught in a hard place since you sell alcohol and you want what is best for both your family and your neighbors [MIA—developing discrepancy]. Would it be OK with you if I shared what some of the other advantages of working in a group might be [MIA]?

STAKEHOLDER: Sure, what are they?

SOCIAL WORKER: Well, for one thing, sometimes organized groups bring together business owners like you to create a large buying pool, to purchase automatic [driver's license] scanners at a reasonable price. That way it would be right on your counter and all your employees would use it. Another benefit, if you decided to participate, might be that group members could help you with looking at other ways to increase profits, by selling merchandise other than alcohol that your neighbors want to buy. And if changes in the laws are suggested, then you would be a part of the decision-making process [GI]. What do you think of that [OQ]?

STAKEHOLDER: (*surprised*) You mean other owners will be there? And other businesspeople? So the focus isn't just on making the laws tougher but on how the group can work together to help people like me and to prevent teen drinking? Well, that's interesting. Yes, if that is the case, <u>I would be willing to come</u>, to at least check it out. When is the meeting?

SOCIAL WORKER: (*Provides the information.*) So I will see you then next Thursday at 7:30 [securing commitment]?

STAKEHOLDER: Yes, I will come. See you then.

In this case scenario, MaryAnn used reflective listening and open questions to learn of Mr. Kamdar's self-interests: to assure profit, to control employees so as not to get in further trouble, to be seen as a respectable business owner in the community, and to keep alcohol problems away from his own teenage son. She provided him with information about the benefits of joining a group/coalition without arguing about why he should join. She listened to his concerns and evoked from him his self-interests or motivators. Coming alongside and her use of double-sided reflections helped to develop discrepancy. As Mr. Kamdar heard himself talk about his motivators and MaryAnn reflected them back, he began to see himself in a somewhat different light. He wanted to be a valuable member of the community, and he wanted his business to keep on being successful. Mr. Kamdar also became more interested as she gave him information about some of the strategies the group might consider that would benefit him directly.

MaryAnn realized she had reached one goal: Mr. Kamdar's commitment to come to a coalition meeting. Next, her goal was to elicit change talk and commitment from all coalition members to work toward a larger commitment. First, the group had to define the problem and then decide what their goals would be. Discussion of methods for achieving those goals would be held after the group/coalition reached a common agreement on the problem.

> MaryAnn realized that working with a group/coalition of different community members with various self-interests might be very difficult. An adviser who had worked with coalitions in the past told her that often store owners, such as Mr. Kamdar, come to the meetings but disrupt them if they feel that the group is moving forward with actions that are seen as negative. In this instance, some of the community members who were interested in attending had already been discussing using organized assessments of bars and liquor stores to make sure they were in compliance with state law. Those that weren't would be turned over to the state licensing board for investigation. MaryAnn was concerned that tightening community oversight and laws might drive store owners away from any involvement. Their participation was essential in developing a holistic plan. Her goal in working with the group was to use MI skills to listen to all members and to focus them on defining the problem. A common problem and goal would need to be reached before the development of a strategy or plan. All members' views would need to be considered. The following dialogue is from her meeting with the group:

SOCIAL WORKER: I want to thank everyone for coming together to discuss ways that we can prevent teenage alcohol use—and related drinking and driving problems—here in our community. I know many of us have different ideas about how we can do this and we all have the common goal of caring about the teenagers who are our children, neighbors, and friends [GI]. Before we begin, I was wondering what you would like to see happen in this meeting [OQ]?

SCHOOL PRINCIPAL: Well, I personally would like to hear from everyone here. I know that each of us has different ideas as to what the problem is and maybe ideas about how to solve it. But we can't fix this problem on our own, and we need to come together as a group to figure this out.

POLICE OFFICER: Yes, I agree. Everyone has a different viewpoint and no one person is the bad guy. It is important that we listen to everyone without arguing.

YOUTH: Everyone's opinions and ideas are important.

SOCIAL WORKER: Coming together as group can help us generate ideas that we might not have thought of on our own, especially if we take the time to listen to each person. Figuring out the problem first will help us to think of solutions later [CR—helping to focus/set agenda].

PARENT 1: Well, you already heard my idea: I think we should get the state to come out to assess these bars and stores and make sure they aren't selling booze to kids. And if we are, we fine them! If we hit them where it hurts, with money, then they might be more likely to not be selling alcohol.

PARENT 2: Yes, the main problem is access. If the teenagers couldn't get alcohol from these places, then there would be no problem.

CLERGY: On the other hand, teens are getting alcohol at home and are drinking there, some with their parents' permission. It isn't just the stores and bars; family members, maybe older siblings are buying it for them as well.

SOCIAL WORKER: Some of the concerns, then, are that teens are getting alcohol from several different places: they may be able to buy it or get their older brothers or sisters to buy it, or maybe they have it served in their homes [SR]. How does this concern you as parent [OQ—elaboration question for evoking change talk; keeping focus on eliciting concerns before strategies]?

PARENT 2: It makes it hard. I have three teenagers and I tell them that they are not allowed to drink. Then they see their friends' parents giving their kids alcohol. I tell them that if they are at a party and alcohol is being served, then they have to come home. Immediately. They listen but complain. And I feel like the bad guy. Why are these other parents putting me in this position? Don't they get it? Why would they give their kids and other people's kids alcohol?

YOUTH LEADER: I'll tell you my concern: there isn't much for kids to do around here. I have organized some basketball tournaments and I am amazed at how many show up. They seem glad to have something to do. So maybe if we, as a group, offered some positive things for kids to do, then they wouldn't be bored and maybe want to go drinking. I want to be able to help. I just can't do everything on my own.

PARENT 1: I don't want any of my kids to be able to buy alcohol, either here or in the next county. I certainly don't provide it for them, and they know I don't approve of their drinking. That is why I am here. They are always complaining about being bored, that there is nothing to do. I want to see if there is something I can do to fix this problem.

SOCIAL WORKER: Some of the concerns are around the availability of alcohol from other parents at parties, you as parents end up looking like you are too strict, and your teens telling you that there is nothing else to do [SR]. What else concerns people about teen drinking [OQ]?

POLICE OFFICER: I was the one who was first on the scene of the drunk driving accident. That was bad, but what was worse was telling the parents that their children had died. I never want to have to do that again, but I know I will have to. Also, arresting underage drinkers takes up a lot of time on the weekends when I could be using my time with more important police matters. Kids think drinking is a rite of passage, but all it does is cause trouble for them and for our department. Of course, alcohol use in adults can cause trouble too, but with the teens there are many more people involved.

MR. KAMDAR: I own a liquor store, and I don't want a bunch of rules or laws to come my way with you all thinking that this will fix the problem. I work at making sure my employees ask for ID from anyone who looks 30 or under. What is hard is when teens come in, in a group, and steal from me. When there is just one employee, or myself working alone, then it is hard to deal with a group of kids. They take the alcohol and run out the door. So I look bad and also lose money. I am interested in addressing this problem, but the problem goes beyond access to alcohol.

SCHOOL PRINCIPAL: I am concerned as we sometimes have drinking problems during the day, on campus. I have had a few students show up to class drunk. Then the teacher has to stop everything, call me, and then I have to call the parents to pick them up. We have a zero tolerance policy, so then the problem gets even bigger. The students have to be suspended. <u>I just want students to be able to come to school</u> and learn and have an environment that supports that.

SOCIAL WORKER: Let me see if I can summarize what everyone has said so far. You see teen drinking as a problem in many areas: teens are getting alcohol at home or they are having their siblings buy it or they steal it from stores; teens who normally wouldn't drink are seeing their friends doing it, sometimes with parental approval, which undermines your role as a parent; your teens tell you that they are bored and there isn't much to do in this community besides drink; some drink in school, which disrupts the learning process; they get into fights and other problems that take up law enforcement's resources or even worse, get into driving fatalities. You all are here for several reasons. You realize that this is a problem that you can't solve on your own, you have a desire to keep youth in this community safe, and to keep this community as a good place to raise families and do business [CR].

MR. KAMDAR: Yes, you are right about that. We have a lot of goals in common, even though we see the problem from our own viewpoints.

In this group meeting, MaryAnn set the stage by asking what each individual wanted to see happen. She strategically reflected the comments that would be consistent with the consensus organizing model—that is, that the meeting be used as a respectful place to hear from all the various stakeholders. The focus of the meeting was on eliciting the concerns and perspectives of each member, and of course, the meeting would last much longer than is suggested in the provided dialogue. Later, other meetings would be held to start developing strategies from the group, and the group may decide to form a more formalized coalition. MaryAnn's role at that point would be to use OARS skills to keep the group focused and to elicit discussion of the benefits and possible problems with the suggested strategies. She could also provide information regarding evidence-based prevention strategies for the group to consider, but ultimately the plan would be up to the group/coalition. Once the group had developed a plan, had assigned members to various tasks, and had made a commitment to that plan, her role would be to act as a resource and support through the provision of affirmations, hope, and optimism. She could also be a resource in seeking out new partners.

FINAL THOUGHTS

Using a client-centered framework of community organizing such as consensus organizing will be helpful to social workers who wish to use MI in this type of work; CO social workers may be interested in learning MI to help them facilitate their discussions with stakeholders. Community coalitions have been found to be very effective regarding decreasing teen alcohol and other drug use, particularly when there are multiple strategies that target existing laws, norms, and practices across a variety of areas (Griffin & Botvin, 2010; Holder et al., 2000; Perry et al., 1996). Bringing together community members who may not normally interact with each other can be challenging; "motivating" them to work together is particularly where MI may prove the most useful.

9

Integrating Motivational Interviewing into Social Work Practice

WITH RHODA EMLYN-JONES, BILL JAMES, AND CRISTINE URQUHART

M I is simple but not easy. Learning MI skills and then using them in a strategic manner takes a good deal of practice. For some of you, this book may be your first exposure to MI; for others, you may have attended beginning and advanced MI workshops and want to learn more. If you are interested in increasing your own MI skills, what is the best way to do this? Some of you may be administrators or managers and are thinking about how you might go about integrating MI agencywide or systemwide, depending on your setting. And if you learn MI yourself and/or want to train it with a group of agency staff, how might you expect MI to change social work practice? And more importantly, what are the effects of using MI spirit and skills with clients?

To answer these questions, we will take a look at what is known about learning MI from training research studies, many of which have involved social workers. I have invited social work practitioners who have worked to train and integrate MI skills and spirit into micro, mezzo, and macro settings to describe their experiences. The goal, if you are interested, is to help you to come up with either an individualized learning plan for yourself, your staff, or your agency.

WHAT IS INVOLVED IN LEARNING MI?

By this point in this book, it has probably become evident that MI has quite a few different components or aspects. Miller and Moyers (2006) indicated that there are eight stages (which are not necessarily sequential) that are important in learning MI: (1) working in the spirit of MI and being collaborative with clients, (2) becoming proficient in OARS skills in order to engage clients, (3) being able to recognize and respond to clients' change talk, (4) having the ability to elicit change talk from clients and guide them toward a behavioral goal, (5) rolling with resistance that may emerge from clients, (6) assisting clients in the planning process, (7) helping clients consolidate a commitment to change, and (8) using and blending MI with other methods of counseling, when necessary. Typically, trainings of MI use both didactic and skill-building practice methods and currently tend to focus more on areas 1–5 with less emphasis on the others (Madson, Loignon, & Lane, 2009). This may be changing as there has been increased interest in offering workshops, for instance, in blending MI with cognitive-behavioral therapy (Carter & Koutsenok, 2010). MINT at this time does not "certify" trainers but puts candidates for their sponsored training for new trainers (TNT) through a rigorous application process designed to ensure that candidates have themselves had sufficient training, experience, and supervisions to develop proficiency in the practice of MI. If you are seeking an MI trainer, MINT trainers in particular geographic areas can be found through *www.motivationalinterviewing.org*.

WHAT THE TRAINING STUDIES TELL US

Training studies of MI have focused on either self-selected, recruited trainees from a variety of disciplines, including social workers, or trainees in specific agency/community settings, such as mental health or probation (Madson, Loignon, & Lane, 2009; Schoener, Madeja, Henderson, Ondersma, & Janisse, 2006). In these studies, MI skill proficiency is usually measured using audiotaped interviews with either real clients or simulated clients (actors). Tapes are coded using objective measures, such as the MI

Skills Code (MISC; Moyers, Martin, Catley, Harris, & Ahluwalia, 2003), which codes both therapist and client speech, or the MI Treatment Integrity (MITI; Moyers, Martin, Manuel, Hendrickson, & Miller, 2005), where only therapist/counselor speech is coded.

In pretraining measures, studies have found that trainees tended to use the "default" method of communication: in these instances, it was little reflective listening (mental health practitioners) or aggressive, confrontational methods (child welfare social workers) (Forrester et al., 2008; Schoener et al., 2006). In posttraining measures, trainees were able to make skill gains when immediately measured after 2-day workshops. For some, it was hard to "unlearn" old habits and remove them from practice, yet other studies have found that trainees are able to reduce their MI-inconsistent behaviors and to meet minimal proficiency levels as established in the MISC and MITI (Madson, Bullock, Speed, & Hodges, 2009; Miller & Mount, 2001; Miller et al., 2004; Schoener et al., 2006).

Several studies have found that there are no demographic, ethnic, educational, or personality characteristics that impact learning MI by community-based practitioners (Baer et al., 2009; Hartzler, Baer, Dunn, Rosengren, & Wells, 2007; Miller et al., 2004, 2008; Mitcheson, Bhavsar, & McCambridge, 2009). A study of "mandated" trainees from juvenile corrections found that level of motivation to use MI at the beginning of training made no difference in skill attainment; however, females with higher education levels tended to do best (Hohman, Doran, & Koutsenok, 2009).

When measured over a period of time after training, MI skills have been found either to be maintained or to have decreased, when trainees have attended an initial workshop only. Providing feedback of audiotape results and scores and coaching over several months or a year tend to have the best outcomes in terms of skill proficiency and maintenance (Miller et al., 2004). Self-assessment of MI skills, when compared to coded audiotapes of interviews, has been found to be overestimated or underestimated. Fluctuations in self-report like this may be due to the context demands of the settings of these studies. Overestimates may be related to mandated trainees wanting to have the assessment of their work over with; underestimates may be due to trainees not wanting to appear overly confident to the "expert" MI trainers who worked with them (Hartzler et al., 2007; Miller & Mount, 2001). A comparison of therapists, supervisors, and objective observers found that while there was some correspondence of tape ratings between the three groups regarding OARS skills, there was less agreement between the supervisors and the observers on the more advanced MI skills, such as eliciting and responding to change talk. Supervisors tended to be more in line with the therapists' ratings, which may be due to positive bias (Martino, Ball, Nich, Frankforter, & Carroll, 2009). While trainees may not be good at estimating their own skill level, perhaps clients can rate their counselor's skills. Interestingly, simulated clients were asked to rate their counselors on six behaviors thought to be representative of the MI spirit. Their ratings were significantly correlated with those of the independent observers (Bennett, Roberts, et al., 2007).

Making audiotapes available for coding, feedback, and coaching is often a difficult process in that trainees have problems with time constraints, work demands, and possibly performance anxiety; thus some don't follow through with submitting tapes. Some trainees think that it can also be difficult to get clients to consent to being taped when that usually is not an issue (Baer et al., 2004; Bennett, Moore, et al., 2007; Forrester et al., 2008; Moyers, Manuel, Wilson, et al., 2007).

Few studies have examined the impact of learning and utilizing MI on how trainees perceive their work. Miller and colleagues (2004) report anecdotally that the trainees from their study (some of whom were social workers) indicated that after learning MI they left their agencies, finding them too authoritarian and in conflict with the spirit of MI. There are other reports that using MI helps to reduce burnout or to feel more empowered (Schoener et al., 2006). In a qualitative study, domestic violence advocates who had been trained in MI reported that using MI made them feel more confident in their work and better able to work with resistant clients, similar to the findings of Forrester and colleagues' (2007) study of child welfare social workers in the United Kingdom (Owen, 2007).

Organizational culture, as indicated above, can provide supports or barriers to adopting the spirit and use of MI. If practitioners perceive that decisions are being made without their input and have little knowledge about what MI entails prior to training, they may be more likely to believe that using MI will add to their workload and will not be as invested in using it. Organizations that have a culture of being open to change and encouraging staff to try new practices are more likely to see gains in MI skill (Baer et al., 2009; Berger, Otto-Salaj, Stoffel, Hernandez-Meier, & Gromoske, 2009).

In terms of the impact of using MI with clients, studies (that compared groups of practitioners who had been trained in MI with those who had not been trained) found increases in change talk and decreases in resistance in the clients of the MI-trained group (Miller et al., 2004; Schoener et al., 2006). Other training studies have reported no difference in client change talk when measured after training (Miller & Mount, 2001). Spiller and

Guelfi (2007) trained social workers in Italy who worked with cannabis users in a mandated program. Clients of the MI-trained social workers were significantly more likely to report experiencing more empathy and less confrontation in their interactions, as compared to the clients who received treatment as usual. The clients were also more likely to report that they had received help to think about their behavior and felt an increased perception that they needed to change. While not a typically studied client outcome, a report of MI training for a cross-discipline unit in a psychiatric hospital found that posttraining, violent incidents on the unit decreased from 3.5 to 2.2 per month (Levy, Ricketts, & Le Blanc, 2010).

DEVELOPING A LEARNING AND INTEGRATION PLAN

Based on these research findings, Table 9.1 provides a guideline for creating MI learning plans at the individual (micro) level, the unit (mezzo) level, or agencywide (macro) level.

Individual Learning Plans

In creating your own individualized learning plan, it is important to go beyond reading books on MI. Attending several community-based trainings or a semester-long university course is helpful in making skill gain; working with an expert MI trainer who provides audiotape coding, feedback, and coaching will help consolidate training gains as well as give opportunities for continued practice under supervision. Anecdotally, trainees report that attending an MITI coding class also increases their own awareness to pay attention to the minute details in their communication with clients.

Self-analysis after sessions with clients may be helpful, but it is recommended that this be done in the context of comparing your work with the analysis of an objective coder or observer. The Practitioner Self-Assessment of MI Interview was created for this purpose (see Figure 9.1; Hartzler et al., 2007). Developed for a research study of community substance abuse treatment counselors ($n = 23$), it provides a format for an individual to self-assess and compare findings with that of a third-party observer. Practitioners are asked to estimate the number of times both they and their clients exhibited specific behaviors, such as used open-ended questions (by the practitioner) or sidetracked the conversation (by the client). They are then asked to rate their confidence in this these estimates so that they can develop better accuracy over time in self-monitoring.

TABLE 9.1. Integration of MI into Social Work Practice: Micro, Mezzo, and Macro

Individual practice	Unit in agency	Agencywide
Basic MI 2- to 4-hour overview	Read MI books/articles	Administration vision and support
Read MI books/articles	Introductory workshop (1–2 days) and advanced workshop (2–3 days)	Input from supervisors, staff, and clients
Introductory workshop (1–2 days) and advanced workshop (2–3 days) or semester-long MI course	Audiotape coding, feedback, and coaching	Logistics planning with MI trainers
	Self-analysis with consultant feedback	Curriculum development
Audiotape coding, feedback, and coaching	Live observation with feedback	Introductory workshop (1–2 days) and advanced workshop (2–3 days)
Self-analysis with consultant feedback	Feedback from clients	Audiotape coding, feedback, and coaching
Live observation with feedback	Clinical supervision and/or peer support groups; use of videos, role plays	Self-analysis with consultant feedback
Feedback from clients		Live observation with feedback
MITI coding workshop	MI supervision workshop	Feedback from clients
	Visual reminders; success stories	MI supervision workshop
	Refresher trainings; new hires familiar with MI	MITI coding workshop
		Clinical supervision and/or peer support groups; use of videos, role plays
		Visual reminders; success stories
		Refresher trainings; new hires familiar with MI
		Policies and procedures to support MI use
		Training of new (internal) trainers
		Implementation teams
		MI integrated into specific services (i.e., intake, case management)

Using the scales provided, rate your performance during the interview:

1. **Empathy** (understanding of client perspective)	1 Low	2	3	4	5 High
2. **MI spirit** (collaborative approach, supporting client autonomy, eliciting of client ideas)	1 Low	2	3	4	5 High
3. **Direction** (persistence of focus on target behavior)	1 Low	2	3	4	5 High

Provide your best estimate for the frequency of these specific interviewer behaviors. If you do not recall an instance of a given behavior, answer "0." Then rate your confidence in each estimate using the scale below.

1	2	3	4	5
Not at all confident		Moderately confident		Very confident

During the interview, how often did you:	Estimate	Confidence Rating				
1. ask your client "closed" questions (e.g., questions that elicit only "yes" or "no" answers)?	times	1	2	3	4	5
2. ask your client "open" questions (e.g., questions that elicit more than "yes" or "no" answers)?	times	1	2	3	4	5
3. repeat or paraphrase your client's statements?	times	1	2	3	4	5
4. summarize or add meaning to client statements?	times	1	2	3	4	5
5. affirm or support your client's ideas?	times	1	2	3	4	5
6. ask permission to provide advice, or emphasize your client's control over decisions?	times	1	2	3	4	5
7. warn or advise your client without permission?	times	1	2	3	4	5
8. confront your client about problems?	times	1	2	3	4	5

Please provide your best estimate for the frequency of these specific client behaviors. If you do not recall an instance of a given behavior, answer "0." Then rate your confidence in each estimate using the scale below.

(*continued*)

FIGURE 9.1. Practitioner Self-Assessment of MI Interview (Hartzler et al., 2007). Copyright 2010 by Bryan Hartzler, PhD, and John Baer, PhD, University of Washington. The authors grant permission to use this instrument for personal use and research purposes, provided that users do not modify it and that proper acknowledgment is given to its source. For permission to use this instrument for commercial purposes, contact Bryan Hartzler, PhD (*hartzb@u.washington.edu*) or John Baer, PhD (*jsbaer@u.washington.edu*). Available at *lib.adai.washington.edu/instruments*.

1	2	3	4	5
Not at all confident		Moderately confident		Very confident

During the interview, how often did your client:	Estimate	Confidence Rating				
1. state a desire for change?	times	1	2	3	4	5
2. suggest an ability to change?	times	1	2	3	4	5
3. specify a reason to change?	times	1	2	3	4	5
4. indicate a need for change?	times	1	2	3	4	5
5. assert a commitment to change?	times	1	2	3	4	5
6. state lack of desire to change?	times	1	2	3	4	5
7. suggest an inability to change?	times	1	2	3	4	5
8. specify a reason to not change?	times	1	2	3	4	5
9. indicate a need to not change?	times	1	2	3	4	5
10. assert a commitment to not change?	times	1	2	3	4	5
11. challenge your ideas or convey hostility?	times	1	2	3	4	5
12. cut you off or speak over you?	times	1	2	3	4	5
13. sidetrack conversation or opt not to respond?	times	1	2	3	4	5
14. blame, excuse, or minimize problems?	times	1	2	3	4	5

FIGURE 9.1. (*continued*)

This measure is a combination of the global scores and behavior count items from the MITI and client change language from the MISC (Hartzler et al., 2007). The observer uses the same form for later feedback to the practitioner. In Hartzler and colleagues' (2007) study of this measure, good interrater reliability among independent raters/observers was found. At the pretest, before 9 weeks of training, coaching, and feedback, trainees' self-assessment had a poor correlation with those of the observers. Trainees were able with some accuracy to rate their own use of open questions and client change talk only. By the end of the study period, they were much more able to identify spirit, closed questions, simple and complex reflections, sustain talk, and MI-adherent behaviors. Again, this indicates that self-assessment skills need to be used in conjunction with other observer feedback but that these skills can improve over time.

Feedback from clients can also provide important information. While you wouldn't ask clients to differentiate a simple from a complex reflection, they can certainly tell you about your interaction with them in general. A feedback measure that has been developed is the Client Evaluation of Motivational Interviewing (CE-MI; Madson, Bullock, Speed, & Hodges, 2009) that can be given to clients to fill out at the end of an interview. Live observation of interactions with feedback may be helpful but certainly not at the level of receiving your own audiotapes transcripted with coding. When I (MH) teach MI in my graduate program, students comment on how they thought they used various MI skills in an interview; listening to their tapes later and looking at a coded transcript have shown them that typically the skill use wasn't at the level they had expected to see. Once you have received proficiency in MI, as designated by the MITI, you still might want to attend a refresher training or submit a tape to your coach every once in awhile to address possible skill drift.

Group or Unit in an Agency

If you are a manager or supervisor and would like your staff to learn and utilize MI, ideally you all would attend MI trainings. If you have the budget, always an issue, taking MI supervision training will also help you utilize MI in your own coaching and work with your staff. Setting up peer group supervision or other group supervision where taped interviews with clients are reviewed and possibly coded (if you have been trained in coding) can be helpful, once you overcome possible performance anxiety. Some supervisors have reported using MI videos and role plays with group analysis, discussion, and critique. A study of MI in the workplace gave trainees (who had completed a 2-day training) 12 weekly worksheets that they used to analyze their own interview tapes, such as by counting the number of complex reflections. These worksheets were followed up by telephone-based coaching based on observer coding (Bennett, Moore, et al., 2007).

The MIA-STEP (Motivational Interviewing Assessment–Supervisory Tools for Enhancing Proficiency) is another model that was developed by the National Institute on Drug Abuse and the Substance Abuse and Mental Health Services Administration to provide substance abuse treatment agencies with a format to train, integrate, and supervise MI. For more information, see *www.attcnetwork.org/explore/priorityareas/science/blendinginitiative/miastep*. This program also contains observation and self-report forms for supervisors and staff. For the supervisor, one of the main challenges may be to "motivate" staff to participate and provide audiotapes for group supervision. Use of visual tools, such as posters and bookmarks, can remind staff to use various MI skills, as well as hearing MI "success" stories.

Agency- or Systemwide

Integrating MI and other evidence-based practices into larger systems of human service work is difficult and has earned its own area of research called implementation science (Fixsen, Naoom, Blase, Friedman, & Wallace, 2005). While it is beyond the scope of this chapter to detail the steps involved in this and other models, much of what is presented in Table 9.1 is congruent with what this particular line of research tells us is important in implementing/integrating any change in practice or skill development.

Administrators at some point make a decision to integrate the use of MI across many units or levels within the agency. The next step is to involve supervisors, practitioners, and perhaps clients in a discussion as to what this might mean in the context of agency culture, their concerns, and to obtain support (Berger et al., 2009). Having had a brief exposure to MI will help with knowledge of at least what is involved with this method of communication. The next step would be to plan logistics of training and involve MI trainers in this process. Questions of who will be trained, when, and whether it should be mandatory or voluntary should all be considered. What will be trained is important as well, and a curriculum to make sure all trainings are uniform will need to be developed (Hohman, Doran, & Koutsenok, 2009).

Trainings are offered and supervisors are trained in the MI supervision and coaching model. Agencies can solicit feedback from clients and/or do live observations; the best way to determine whether MI is being used as designed is to use a fidelity instrument (Fixsen et al., 2005), which is the MITI coding system. Ideally, staff or a select group of staff, provides taped interviews for coding over time, so that they can continue in their skill development. As in the unit learning plan, peer groups and/or supervision groups can use role plays and videos for continued learning. All of these should be supported by policies and procedures that support this integration, from promoting a culture in the agency that is based on the spirit of MI to allowing the use of work time for peer group supervision. As internal trainers are trained in MI, they will allow for continued training in-house to sustain the skill growth. Implementation teams can provide structure for many of these changes as well as design how MI skills can be used specifically in the agency, such as a part of every intake interview. Bookmarks with MI skills listed or posters can be placed throughout the agency as visual reminders. Certainly, sharing MI success stories helps to build the self-efficacy of practitioners in its use. Periodic or refresher training can be provided, and hiring practitioners who have experience with MI or are open to learn it will help build sustainability of the integration.

EXPERIENCES FROM THE FIELD

The following are accounts given by three social workers regarding their work with integrating MI into their own or agency practice.

Micro/Mezzo: Bill James, San Diego, California

I work in Child Welfare Services (CWS) as a supervisor. My staff works with foster youth (ages 15–18) who require group home or treatment-level Foster Family Agency (FFA) placement. This means my staff ends up having long-term relationships with young clients who are usually at risk for a variety of dangerous behaviors. The youth generally need to stay engaged in mental health and educational services while in foster care. Since I started working in CWS in 1993, I have been listening to peers, and occasionally myself, argue with clients around a variety of issues at some of the most vulnerable times those clients will ever face in their lives. And for years, in order to avoid this dynamic, I tried not to needlessly antagonize clients while helping them navigate the CWS system. In 2006, on the advice of a friend in the field, I attended an overview and introduction to MI. I walked out of that training utterly convinced that the lives of our clients and the well-being of my staff would be significantly better if I could integrate MI into our casework practice.

I then approached my manager about my desire to teach MI skills to my staff and he readily agreed to this. My first challenge, however, was to develop my own competency in MI. A large mental health agency in the area had committed to bringing MI practice to all of their staff, and they were generous enough to let me attend several of their trainings. One of their supervisors traded "guest appearances" in our respective group supervision sessions over several months. I sought out a member of MINT who agreed to code my own audiotapes and provide me feedback and coaching over a period of about 6 months.

In turn, I began to work with my own staff in group supervision using written materials, training videos, and my own attempts to explain and model MI. We all participated in many "real" plays, which we recorded and coded together. At first, my very patient staff didn't do very well. I relied heavily on video examples and spent too much time trying to talk them through the process. I also met with each of them individually to assess their ability to reflect and guide conversations. I learned that I had to use MI skills in the training process which included evoking from my staff their thoughts and ideas of how to use MI. The best progress has been through regular monthly meetings focused on MI skill building, sharing success stories, and sorting through difficult cases. The process was improved by having the supervisor of another unit that works with the same population commit to wanting his staff to learn MI, so there are often 7–10 social workers at any one time in our group meetings, as well as the other supervisor. This broadens the number of MI-use success stories available to talk about and the problem-solving options that staff can come up with.

Perhaps the most important lesson we have learned together is recognizing the limits of MI and knowing when to switch to some other skill or strategy. Being held responsible by the courts, as well as feeling personally responsible, for the well-being of foster youth is a burden that weighs heavily on social workers. We must deal with a variety of issues in clients' lives beyond the consideration of behavior change. Beyond MI, at times we have to make and communicate to them and their families decisions about where our clients will live, where they will go to school, whether or not visitation with their family will be supervised, how we find them when they run away, how we work with law enforcement to catch those who abuse them, and dozens of other issues. Even with understanding the realities of our dual roles, my staff must sometimes "make peace" with the idea that they may have to occasionally walk away from an interaction involving problematic behavior without making a dent in a foster youth's intent to continue with that behavior. Because of all of these other issues, sometimes using MI is not enough. This has been *very* difficult.

One important lesson I encountered was that each of my staff was on very different learning curves. They each have unique styles of learning and have varying levels of motivation to even consider trying to incorporate a different style of communication. This is not unique to CWS of course, but becoming sophisticated in the ways of adult learning theory was not something I anticipated when I started this process (not that I am there yet!). The challenge I face in implementing MI in my unit is overcoming the belief that the traditional confrontational/ argumentative methods of communicating "work," since over half of all the children in the foster care system do return home to their parents. And while the skills involved in MI are clearly teachable, making reflective statements, strategically directing a conversation, and resisting the righting reflex is not a natural way to interact with others on a day-to-day basis. Lastly, many of the social workers I supervise with do not consider themselves "clinical" social workers, so the idea that I would ask them to hone micro interview skills was rather foreign to them. This cultural bias in my agency seems even more entrenched in other sections and regions among supervisory staff. I gather that this is a similar dynamic to reactions in the criminal justice system, but worth taking into account when approaching a CWS workforce.

There have been several positive results from this whole process. The first is that several of my staff report that they feel less anxiety when confronted with highly resistant clients because they have tools that seem to make the encounter less confrontational in the moment. They also report that they have a better understanding of appropriate roles and responsibilities between themselves and their clients. I can assure you, I wear these expressions of relief like jewels strung on an invisible necklace of supervision accomplishments! A second result is that at least a few of our foster youth have considered or made positive behavior changes over the last few years. I do not think they would have normally done this were it not for a more effective approach by my staff. A third result is that the idea that MI could help in CWS work is catching on slowly with my peers and with some in administration. My manager agreed to use some of his hard-won training dollars to send several staff to outside MI training in an effort to make the skills more available to his entire section. And finally, and perhaps most importantly, I have become a better supervisor by utilizing the spirit and OARS skills of MI. I have been able to focus my attention on the strengths and talents my own staff brings to the table when there are problems and issues that need to be addressed, either as a unit as a whole or in their own work habits or caseload.

Mezzo/Macro: Cristine Urquhart, Vancouver, British Columbia, Canada

My connection with MI is an ever evolving long-term relationship that began in 1996 while I was researching alcohol interventions. In the 15 years since, MI has influenced many of my educational and professional decisions. I studied and worked at institutions where MI was valued and practiced, and made it a focus of my clinical training for my MSW. I had always felt that there had to be another way of understanding and working with people with substance use concerns, beyond all-or-nothing labeling and shaming approaches. It didn't make sense to me that people had to completely lose everything (hit bottom) before they could get help. MI offered a way of working with people bringing humanity, dignity, and hope to the relationship. It completely made sense to me, and I found it to be the fit I was looking for to support people with complex health and social concerns and to practice social work.

Sometimes agencywide change begins when opportunities coalesce, doors open, and vision, boldness, and lived experiences create critical mass. This was my experience, along with that of Frances Jasiura, as an MI co-trainer and consultant with Addiction Services, Annapolis Valley Health (AS, AVH), in Nova Scotia, Canada. AVH administrators had become concerned that many clients with substance use and gambling problems never access specialized addiction treatment services, utilizing other health areas such as primary care instead. The agency wanted to shift to integrated levels of service that were collaborative and empowering for clients. This culture change was further supported by a national framework recently proposed by the Canadian government regarding substance use treatment.

The district manager of AS had been struck by the spirit of MI when he attended a training that was led by Bill Miller several years earlier, and saw how autonomy, respect, and evocation were linked to the emerging changes that were occuring in treatment culture. He successfully accessed one-time funding to offer multilevel MI training for all of Addiction Services staff (community-based, structured treatment, withdrawal management; 32 total staff, including seven social workers), and spread the net wider by inviting community partners, such as mental health, public health and probation services.

The following describes our experience supporting engagement through multilevel training, integrating MI within AS-AVH, and strengthening capacities with virtual coaching and MI Communities of Practice (CoPs). Some of the barriers and supports for integration and considerations for other agencies will also be shared.

Drawing on the research on how to learn MI, we recommended a multilevel approach to support skill development and sustainability. The goals of the training, as identified by the agency, were to build capacity in MI skills, work collaboratively across disciplines, and increase the confidence of nonspecialists to begin conversation around substance use and gambling. We also proposed the development of sustainable MI Communities of Practice (MI CoPs)—shared interest, peer-led learning groups—to strengthen fidelity to MI and support the paradigm shift in the agency.

The training was held between June and December 2010. To accommodate the tremendous interest of community partners, each level of training was repeated. To date, 139 participants have completed the 2-day Level 1 Introductory training, 51 have completed the smaller and more concentrated 2-day Level 2 Advanced, and 46 have signed up for the three 1½-hour follow-up virtual coaching sessions. Currently one virtual coaching session is complete, with a 70% attendance rate. *MI Communities of Practice* are also underway.

It was important to establish system support from the outset. The vice president of Community Health and Continuing Care, and the district manager of Addiction Services welcomed the group and expressed their commitment to the importance of the training, agency integration, and interdisciplinary collaboration. Of interest, 100% of the AS staff attended the Level 1 training. As the training moved forward, it became evident that a few of the participants were ambivalent about being there for historical reasons related to change within the agency. Once this was recognized, we rolled with resistance and stressed that the training was voluntary (MI diffuses by the spirit of MI, not coercion), and asked management to support the same message.

At the start of the Level 2 Advanced training, clear communication was essential to ensure that participants, their managers, and community partners could make informed decisions and renewed commitment every step along the way. In consultation with management, we outlined in writing the following considerations to support engagement in the Advanced training: (1) participants were voluntary and supported by management; (2) they had taken the Level 1 training; (3) they were willing to fully participate in experiential learning, including taping and coding a conversation; (4) they committed to participating in three 1½-hour virtual coaching sessions posttraining; and (5) they were willing to engage in a MI CoP. Overall, 63% of AS staff participated in the Level 2 training.

We introduced measuring MI fidelity and coding in the Level 2 training. Participants were asked to tape and code an MI conversation with a peer. This usually evokes anxiety and, at times, resistance. Knowing this, we made every effort to enhance engagement, increase safety, and reduce barriers. Addiction Services provided the recording equipment that could also later be used in MI CoPs. We encouraged trainees to choose their own partner the day before the taping. Time was provided within the training for the exercise, and the MI interview was brief. Every participant in Level 2 training completed this exercise, and several reported afterward how helpful they found the practice.

As questions arise in daily practice, coaching sessions posttraining were offered to provide ongoing support and skill integration. In small groups, we meet with participants once monthly, for 3 months, by phone and computer for 1½ hours of virtual coaching. Generally, three agreed-upon topics are covered in this time (elicited from participants prior to session and during check-in), with time allotted to role-play, which provided us the opportunity to offer feedback via the "chat" capacity. To support engagement at this stage, we offered choice around date and time, and had sign-up sheets available before the end of Level 2. Forty-six of the 51 Level 2 participants signed up. We also included a scaling question on the Level 2 evaluation regarding commitment to participate in the virtual coaching sessions. The average response ($n = 42$) on a scale of 0–10 was 8.83. When asked what would help affirm/increase their commitment, participants indicated that the sessions needed to be useful, that their time needed to be supported by management, and that they needed opportunity to practice. The first virtual coaching session had a 70% participation rate, of which 34% were AS staff.

Throughout the smaller Level 2 trainings, we worked to strengthen a sense of community among participants and chose learning practices easily translatable to MI CoPs, such as coding DVD clips and transcripts, partner practice, and team consults. Time was allotted for participants to consider how they might organize themselves as they moved forward into their own learning communities. Given the rural nature of the services, the decision was made to organize into three geographical groups, rather than population specific. With the support and assistance of the Project Lead, all three CoPs have met at least once. One group is meeting every 2 weeks to get started, and others are meeting monthly. Generally, the CoPs run 1½ hours and focus on MI successes and challenges, strategy review, and skills practice. As trainers, we strongly encouraged inclusion of a substantial practice component in the sessions; otherwise, the usefulness of the communities could diminish. One group described their ambivalence around practicing, "We found it a bit hard starting the practice AND we found it harder to stop than start."

An ongoing challenge as agencies integrate practice changes is to balance competing workload priorities and time and resource limitations. For those working with community partners, there may be a discrepancy among services in terms of commitment to ongoing connection and learning through CoPs. A mixed response is to be expected. Within AS, some staff have become MI champions, and a minority of others are not engaged. Overall, the Project Lead notes, "MI language and concepts are finding their way into conversations during staff meetings." In terms of relationships with community partners, she explains that "not all of the relationships are lasting. Some folks have disappeared, back into the one-off mode, not receiving the support from their managers for the ongoing participation we asked for. But those who remain engaged are really engaged."

Many factors have influenced the success of integrating MI within AS and with community partners. We believe that none of this would have been possible without visible support from the administration and district manager with vision, passion for MI and "doing it right," along with the resources to make it happen. The support of the Project Lead and her unwavering commitment were essential at all levels, including maintaining momentum and connection with training participants. Also, having 2½ hours of meeting time with the regional Leadership Team, that included management and directors from the community partners, increased system-wide support. Offering the training and CoPs on work time and outlining clear expectations for both participants and management also supported the integration. Participants noted how helpful it was to have something in writing to take to their managers to ensure clear communication. Encouraging the participants' choice each step of the way and supporting ongoing MI CoPs that would meet their learning and practice needs seemed essential.

Although it is still early, the forecast is hopeful. AS-AVH has already invested tremendous energy, passion, and resources into integrating MI within their agency and with community partners. The critical mass is building, and there is a synergy between what MI can offer and the vision for improved health services. It is clear that for MI to be successfully integrated within agencies, the process must be engaging and collaborative, and system support is paramount in terms of time, resources, and overall commitment to sustained change. In the words of the Project Lead, "Implementing MI is a process which requires vision, time and creative ideas for keeping it on everybody's minds. It would be very easy to slip back to pre-MI ways, without serious investment in sustaining it.... It's big-picture thinking."

[Thank you to Frances Jasiura, Kevin Fraser, Shaughney Aston, and Katrina Crosby.]

Macro: Rhoda Emlyn-Jones, Cardiff, Wales, United Kingdom

In 1984, as a social worker within Cardiff social services, I was given the post of alcohol service development officer. I was responsible for two and a half team members, a small set of offices in the city center, and the job of developing alcohol services across the city. By 1986 we had expanded our services. A neighboring county wanted us to provide similar services for them, and we opened a separate center to be accessible to a larger geographical area. The range of services grew to include all substances, legal and illegal, and a variety of functions, counseling services, social work teams, reentry from prison services, drug intervention programs within the criminal justice provision, homeless services, and in the last 10 years, the development of a range of MI-based family-focused services.

Around us in Adult Social Services the culture was moving more toward approaches dominated by assessment, which often resulted in testing the seriousness of the case against the ever rising thresholds. That is, if you, as a client, couldn't prove you were bad enough, you couldn't get a service. Treatment or care planning followed, with plans often issued to the client as plans they had to comply with. They were often based on addressing their deficits rather than building on clients' competencies. The final stage was monitoring—testing whether clients were succeeding in achieving and sustaining change. Expert assessments, deficit-focused care plans, and monitoring: a recipe designed to increase resistance, waste the resources of the service user, and create dependency.

We were not interested in testing motivation or persuading people of the value of change. What we were interested in was lowering natural resistance in clients, exploring their ambivalence, and enabling people to reach a level of hope and determination to challenge and change their lives. In this field so many of our service users are noticed more for the problems they cause than for the problems they face. They are often confronted and challenged to acknowledge the worst thing they have ever done, a debilitating experience for anyone to have. This profoundly affected them when our aspirations were to offer rehabilitative services.

Many social workers feel they are been driven to assess, plan, and monitor, and they feel ill equipped to engage, collaborate, and focus on outcomes. In training they have said to me that without the MI model and skills, we end up being "too nice" or "too nasty." We need to develop a shared approach that grows self-efficacy and autonomy in individuals and families. Not everyone can achieve change, but we as professionals must be true to a process that has the best evidence of effectiveness. We need to support the skills in our staff to engage with people and view them as resourceful, to see people as part of the solution.

All of my services have a shared platform created by the principles that underpin them and the approach they take. Each service we offer shares an aim, which is to maximize the potential for change to the benefit of the individuals, the families, and the communities they serve. We hold MI spirit, principles, and skills at the heart of the service design and delivery. I was free to develop all the services from "day one" and worked to enable consistency and depth in terms of embedding the approach into the fabric of the service culture and approach. Every element of the service was designed to maximize the likelihood of engagement and collaboration, building hope, optimism, and commitment. I provided evidence to my senior officers about the value of the MI approach, and they supported me in embedding this evidenced-based approach into the fabric of our work. They were further convinced by the evidence of effectiveness we were showing. My chief officers observed that this was an efficient and effective way of working that produced good outcomes and achieved excellent feedback from service users. Thus they allowed me to continue to grow more services based on the MI approach.

We continued to train every one of our new workers, whatever their role and function, in MI skills. The spirit and principles underpinning MI became the accepted principles of the whole organization, and the spirit was upheld within the culture of the teams. We developed a training team to deliver MI training to a wide variety of other professionals and organizations outside of our own. Over time we had one of the largest teams of MI trainers anywhere in the world. We created a specialist role in training others in MI. We consolidated learning through ongoing supervision and support. In order to provide this as a free service, we applied for government grants so that we could reach out to services that, if trained and supported, could play a crucial role in assisting in behavior change.

In MI we are interested in engagement, or how can we help the person or family overcome the fears and deep ambivalence that can prevent them from utilizing our services. We are interested in collaboration or having a partnership where clients are recognized as the experts in their own lives. They explore their competencies and their values to assist them in challenging and changing their lives. We are interested in outcomes, not monitoring plans, and knowing together what autonomy looks like and when it has been achieved.

We were often at odds with the wider culture; we needed to share and support our common approach in order to maintain our position. All of our staff apply the MI principles and skills to their wide range of functions: administrators, in the tone of their letters; the way staff answer the phone or meet and greet at reception; the data that are collected and the way they are gathered; as well as within all the different functions of the skilled practitioners from support staff to social workers, counselors, and managers. We are congruent. We are clear that this congruent approach gives the best opportunity for each and every person we come into contact with.

In terms of family-focused interventions, the MI approach is essential. In this country the family or the social network had been disaggregated and deconstructed; services have focused instead on the different and separate interests of men, women, and children. In child protection, workers had been encouraged to communicate about concerns rather than needs, resulting in higher resistance, less engagement, and paradoxically therefore more risk to the children. In my services, we have built family services and trained staff in MI. We focus on engagement skills to respectfully enable families to address the natural discomfort that emanates from the tension between their values, hopes, and aspirations and their family functioning. This uncomfortable feeling becomes what I call "the grit of change" and can only be reached within truly respectful and empathic relationships. Effective services need to focus on empathy and the exploration of cognitive dissonance. One does not work without the other, but enabling people to experience both provides the best opportunity for people to challenge and change their lives. Starting with a shared ideology or understanding of how people change, equipping staff with the best communication skills to explore change, and setting these skilled staff within strong and empowering social services is, in my opinion, the future for effective, efficient, high-quality public services.

FINAL THOUGHTS

The three narratives from "MI champions" demonstrate how MI is being integrated across various levels of social services. Systems theory tells us that systems fight change and work to achieve homeostasis (Kirst-Ashman & Hull, 2009), which in social services is often the "default" method of communication. It takes work to make radical changes, especially as an individual, a group, or a system goes from being experts to collaborators and from advising to eliciting. We want to keep going back to our old, comfortable ways.

As can be seen, fidelity to MI is critical beginning at the micro level in order to truly bring about real skill and practice change. Individuals need motivation to learn, to practice, and to be vulnerable by doing this with colleagues, particularly if they choose to utilize peer learning groups or communities of practice. Integrating MI into a unit in an agency needs administration/management support along with these opportunities for training and continued practice, feedback, and coaching. Systemwide integration can bring about a culture change, or perhaps it is the culture shift that is already occurring in a treatment system that makes it open to learning and utilizing MI. To have fidelity to MI in a system means that all aspects of that system reflect the spirit of MI in their approach to clients which can radically change how our everyday practice is implemented.

We have research that tells us that MI is effective across a variety of problems, as tested in both research-study contexts and community-based agencies (Lundahl, Kunz, Tollefson, Brownell, & Burke, 2010). We are only just beginning to learn how integrating MI into social work practice changes how clients experience our work, the impacts this has on us, and the culture in our agencies. It looks like integrating MI can have far-reaching effects.

10

Final Thoughts

Lessons Learned from Training
and Teaching Motivational Interviewing

Research has informed us about aspects of training that are important to learning MI, as we saw in Chapter 9 (Baer et al., 2009; Madson, Loignon, & Lane, 2009; Miller et al., 2004), and there is other research regarding training/teaching methods such as use of distance learning (Shafer, Rhode, & Chong, 2004). My own work has changed as a result of learning MI. My goal here in sharing it is to provide some insight for those who would like to train or teach MI.

While working as a therapist years ago, I was given the opportunity to teach community college classes in the evenings for students studying to be substance abuse counselors. To continue teaching in this system, I had to complete a course on adult education which I found immensely helpful. When I later enrolled in a social work doctoral program, I found that there were no required courses on teaching; most social work educators are expected to take their practice and research-based knowledge and ably transmit it to their students (East & Chambers, 2007). I was grateful for my community college experience when I began teaching at the university level.

The courses I taught for a few years included research, human development, and substance abuse treatment, and I integrated content on MI into the later course. As timing would have it, I attended the MI TNT workshop in early January 1999, right before I was to begin the semester of teaching two sections of a counseling skills practice class to undergraduate social work students. This workshop is not about MI per se but focuses on increasing skills to be a good MI trainer. It provides trainees with methods and practice on how to structure exercises for learning MI skills, from setup to implementation to debriefing trainees, all done with the spirit of MI. Now I not only knew what to teach but I knew *how* to teach it—again, something that is not usually included in faculty training (Gillingham, 2008).

Learning and teaching MI has transformed my teaching style. Students expect faculty to come to class with their powerpoints and provide lectures on the material that is to be covered in class that day. Like clients who become passive in assessment-driven services, students are passive learners in this method. In turn, they regurgitate what they have learned either on exams or in papers. And students do learn this way (Abel & Campbell, 2009), but for both the instructor and the student, this is not a very interesting or engaging process. I would say that my teaching style before I learned MI was somewhere in between a teacher-centered model (as described previously) and a student-centered one, which is where students take all responsibility for what they want to learn and how they want to learn it (Abel & Campbell, 2009).

Meanwhile, in the community I began to train MI workshops, using the methods and skills that I was taught. I also utilized them in the classroom, at least when I was teaching MI. One of the hallmarks of a good MI trainer is that he or she is able to demonstrate the model, including both the spirit of MI and the technical skills. As client-centered theory and self-determination theory pervaded more of my thinking and I got more experience modeling MI, I found myself using fewer powerpoint slides. I assumed that students had knowledge and experience, even my younger undergraduates, and I worked to draw out from them what they already knew, or thought, or wondered about, even when the topic had nothing to do with MI.

Just as sometimes clients can be a bit puzzled when their social worker interacts with them by using MI ("All I want is someone to just tell me what to do!" a client may state), so can students or community social workers who are trainees be surprised by MI methods. They are looking for someone to provide them with information about the topic of the workshop,

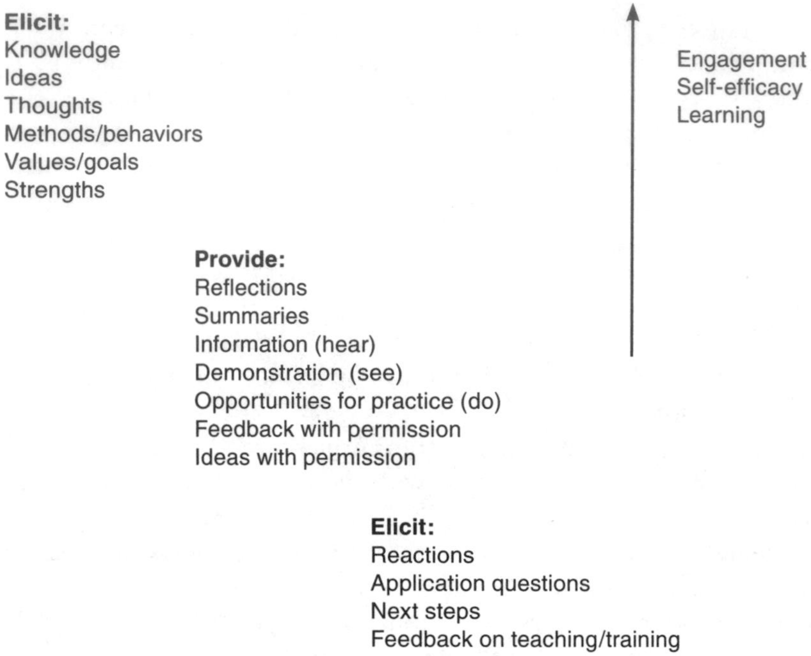

Elicit:
Knowledge
Ideas
Thoughts
Methods/behaviors
Values/goals
Strengths

Engagement
Self-efficacy
Learning

Provide:
Reflections
Summaries
Information (hear)
Demonstration (see)
Opportunities for practice (do)
Feedback with permission
Ideas with permission

Elicit:
Reactions
Application questions
Next steps
Feedback on teaching/training

FIGURE 10.1. A model for training or teaching MI.

and they sit expectantly, waiting to take notes. I developed a model of MI teaching methods (Figure 10.1) to provide a framework for my students, trainees, and myself, of the methods that I use. While it is beyond the scope of this book to examine various adult learning theories, I am sharing a framework that seems to work for me.

Using the elicit–provide–elicit (EPE) model (Rollnick, Miller, & Butler, 2008), I begin by eliciting from students/trainees what they already know about the topic. What are their experiences? perspectives? How do they work with clients now? What do they think is important about this topic? How does it fit into social work practice? There are many different ways to learn about our students' thoughts, values, goals, strengths—the list could go on. This sets the stage that the classroom or workshop will be a collaborative learning experience. We will all learn from one another. As I ask these open-ended questions, I respond with the other OARS skills. Like our clients, students are hearing themselves think out loud. This promotes engagement—that this will be a setting where everyone's ideas are valued and that students/trainees are encouraged to participate.

As a trainer or teacher, while I am often guiding a discussion, sometimes I am still needed to provide some information. Different aspects or points can be made within the discussion that is being elicited. Because we all learn in different ways, it is helpful to hear the information (i.e., "what is reflective listening"), then perhaps see it demonstrated, and then practice it in role or real-plays (dyad interviews using one's own concerns). It is very typical in MI trainings to frequently have exercises and other opportunities to practice the various skills. As our students practice MI skills or whatever skills we are teaching, we can provide affirmations, coaching, feedback, and the like. All of this should be done with permission, something that often takes students aback and is sometimes hard to remember to do. I have to resist my "correcting reflex"! I tend to utilize the EPE model while coaching as well:

Elicit how students/trainees experienced their practice of MI skills:

- "What did you learn in this exercise?"
- "How did you do?"
- "If you had to do it over again, what would you do differently?"
- "What do you need to work on to improve your skills?"
- "What was it like to be the 'client' in this interaction?"
- "What was it like to be the 'social worker'?"
- "How did you respond as the 'client'?"

The *provide* part may be to provide a reflection of what they said, or an affirmation, information, or feedback of what was observed, all done with permission. For example, I might remark:

- "You really had good eye contact and nonverbal communication with your partner."
- "If it is OK with you, I can tell you what saw happen. You tended to raise your voice at the end of your sentences, making the really good reflections you had sound like questions."
- "[after asking for permission to provide feedback] You followed up your reflection with a closed question; you said, 'Is this right?' after giving a wonderful reflection."

I *elicit* their reactions to the material, the practice, the demonstrations, the feedback from a direct observation—whatever we have done. Students might be asked to apply what they have learned to their work with clients or think about how they can integrate and use the new skill. Like asking a client for a commitment, I sometimes ask my trainees:

- "What are your next steps?"
- "What will you work on this next week? How will you work on it?"
- "And, the next week: How did it go?"

Finally, feedback from students or trainees is very important to maintain the collaborative environment and for the trainer/teacher to respond to students' needs. Gillingham (2008, p. 488) proposes a model of obtaining weekly written feedback from students, using Brookfield's (1995) Critical Incident Questionnaire. It is similar to what many MI trainers use at the end of each training day:

- "When did you feel the most engaged in what was happening in class today?"
- "When did you feel the most distanced in what was happening in class today?"
- "What did you find the most affirming and helpful?"
- "What did you find the most puzzling or confusing?"
- "What surprised you the most?"

Many of the methods I use are not new to social work education (Abel & Campbell, 2009), and I attempt to use other skills that are linked to being an effective teacher, such as being organized and having content knowledge (East & Chambers, 2007). Knowing the contexts of trainees' practice or students' internship sites and linking what is learned to those contexts is also helpful and individualizes application. Other aspects of being an effective teacher are those that also make a good MI practitioner: being motivating, encouraging, relational, respectful, and keeping pace with students (Edwards & Richards, 2002; Lowman, 1996). Sounds a lot like MI spirit to me.

FUTURE DIRECTIONS

Learning and using MI is an ongoing process. New knowledge about the use of MI in different settings (micro, mezzo, and macro), with different populations, and in combination with other therapies is constantly being produced. Another direction of research exploration is understanding the mechanism of how MI works (Miller & Rose, 2009). We now know that use of both MI skills and spirit are instrumental in evoking change talk from clients that is related actual change (Moyers et al., 2009). Future studies may focus on understanding this even further by examining and determining what exactly are the essential ingredients in MI in motivating clients toward change. Bill Miller and Steve Rollnick are currently in the process of updating their book (2002), integrating new concepts and research findings from the past decade. The MINT organization is determining the best way to develop new MI trainers as well as standards for training.

The concepts of MI and its use have grown and changed over the years, from being an effective intervention for those with alcohol problems to using it to address a variety of health and other behavioral concerns. Social work practitioners have embraced MI as it fits so well with the ethics and values of our profession and provides an evidence-based method for communication. It can be applied across the various domains and aspects of our work.

I hope that you have found this book helpful. For readers new to MI, perhaps you now feel that this is something that you would like to learn more about. For those already familiar with MI, my goal was for you to look at MI through the eyes of our profession and think about its applications in various settings, some of which are still new to the use of MI. Perhaps you will find some new contexts and interesting uses for MI that have yet to be explored. As you practice and grow in your MI skills, you may find that you approach your work differently. While never specifically studied as to how MI impacts "burnout" or "compassion fatigue," there are some suggestions that using MI can be helpful in these areas (Fahy, 2007). Believing that clients can and will make positive choices and working with them from an egalitarian stance lessens our sense of being the ones who are responsible for changing them. Our work is centered around empowering them, guiding them to find their own answers. Time and time again MI trainers hear anecdotal reports from trainees, that as they integrate MI into their work they find that they have more positive interactions with their clients and look forward to their work with them. Give it a try and see what happens.

References

Abel, E. M., & Campbell, M. (2009). Student-centered learning in an advanced social work practice course: Outcomes of a mixed method investigation. *Social Work Education, 28,* 3–17.

Alinsky, S. D. (1971). *Rules for radicals.* New York: Random House.

Alliance for Excellent Education (2008). *The high cost of high school dropouts: What the nation pays for inadequate high schools.* Washington, DC: Author.

Amrhein, P. C. (2004). How does motivational interviewing work? What client talk reveals. *Journal of Cognitive Psychotherapy: An International Quarterly, 18,* 323–336.

Amrhein, P. C., Miller, W. R., Yahne, C. E., Paler, M., & Fulcher, L. (2003). Client commitment language during motivational interviewing predicts drug use outcomes. *Journal of Consulting and Clinical Psychology, 71,* 862–878.

Anez, L. M., Silva, M. A., Paris, M., & Bedregal, L. E. (2008). Engaging Latinos through the integration of cultural values and motivational interviewing principles. *Professional Psychology, 39,* 153–159.

Apodaca, T. R., & Longabaugh, R. (2009). Mechanisms of change in motivational interviewing: A review and preliminary evaluation of the evidence. *Addiction, 104,* 705–715.

Arkowitz, H., Westra, H. A., Miller, W. R., & Rollnick, S. (2008). *Motivational interviewing in the treatment of psychological problems.* New York: Guilford Press.

Ashton, M. (2005). The motivational hallo. *Drug and Alcohol Findings, 13,* 23–30.

Atkinson, C., & Woods, K. (2003). Motivational interviewing strategies for disaffected secondary school students: A case example. *Educational Psychology in Practice, 19,* 49–64.

Babor, T. F., McRee, B. G., Kassebaum, P. A., Grimaldi, P. L., & Bray, J. (2007). Screening, brief intervention, and referral to treatment (SBIRT): Toward a public health approach to the management of substance abuse. In R. Saitz & M. Galanter (Eds.), *Alcohol/drug screening and brief intervention: Advances in evidence-based practice* (pp. 7–30). Birmingham, NY: Haworth Medical Press.

Baer, J. S., Beadnell, B., Garrett, S. B., Hartzler, B., Wells, E. A., & Peterson, P. L. (2008). Adolescent change language within a brief motivational intervention and substance use outcomes. *Psychology of Addictive Behaviors, 22,* 570–575.

Baer, J. S., Garrett, S. B., Beadnell, B., Wells, E. A., & Peterson, P. (2007). Brief motivational intervention with homeless adolescents: Evaluating effects on substance use and service utilization. *Psychology of Addictive Behaviors, 21,* 582–586.

Baer, J. S., Rosengren, D. B., Dunn, C. W., Wells, E. A., Ogle, R. L., & Hartzler, B. (2004). An evaluation of workshop training in motivational interviewing for addiction and mental health clinicians. *Drug and Alcohol Dependence, 73,* 99–106.

Baer, J. S., Wells, E. A., Rosengren, D. B., Hartzler, B., Beadnell, B., & Dunn, C. (2009). Agency context and tailored training in technology transfer: A pilot evaluation of motivational interviewing training for community counselors. *Journal of Substance Abuse Treatment, 37,* 191–202.

Bandura, A. (1994). Self-efficacy. In V. S. Ramachaudran (Ed.). *Encyclopedia of human behavior* (Vol. 4, pp. 71–81). New York: Academic Press.

Bandura, A. (1999). *Self-efficacy: Toward a unifying theory of behavioral change.* New York: Psychological Press.

Barrett-Lennard, G. T. (1981). The empathy cycle: Refinement of a nuclear concept. *Journal of Counseling Psychology, 28,* 91–100.

Befort, C. A., Nollen, N., Ellerbeck, E. F., Sullivan, D. K., Thomas, J. L., & Ahluwalia, J. S. (2008). Motivational interviewing fails to improve outcomes of a behavioral weight loss program for obese African American women: A pilot randomized trial. *Journal of Behavioral Medicine, 31,* 367–377.

Bem, D. J. (1972). Self-perception theory. In L. Berkowitz (Ed.), *Advances in experimental social psychology* (Vol. 6, pp. 1–62). New York: Academic Press.

Bennett, G. A., Moore, J., Vaughan, T., Rouse, L., Gibbins, J. A., Thomas, P., et al. (2007). Strengthening motivational interviewing skills following initial training: A randomized trial of workplace-based reflective practice. *Addictive Behaviors, 32,* 2963–2975.

Bennett, G. A., Roberts, H. A., Vaughan, T. E., Gibbins, J. A., & Rouse, L. (2007). Evaluating a method of assessing competence in motivational interviewing: A study using simulated patients in the United Kingdom. *Addictive Behaviors, 32,* 69–79.

Berger, L., Otto-Salaj, L. L., Stoffel, V. C., Hernandez-Meier, J., & Gromoske, A. N. (2009). Barriers and facilitators of transferring research to practice: An exploratory case study of motivational interviewing. *Journal of Social Work Practice in the Addictions, 9,* 145–162.

Bernstein, E., Bernstein, J., Feldman, J., Fernandez, W., Hagan, M., Mitchell, P., et al. (2007). The impact if screening, brief intervention, and referral to treatment on emergency department patients' alcohol use. *Annals of Emergency Medicine, 50*(6), 699–710.

Blos, P. (1966). *On adolescence: A psychoanalytic interpretation.* New York: Free Press.

Borrelli, B., McQuaid, E. L., Novak, S. P., Hammond, S. K., & Becker, B. (2010). Motivating Latino caregivers of children with asthma to quit smoking: A randomized trial. *Journal of Consulting and Clinical Psychology, 78* (1), 34–43.

Boust, S. J., Kuhns, M. C., & Studer, L. (2005). Assertive community treatment. In C. E. Stout & R. A. Hayes (Eds.), *The evidence-based practice: Methods, models and tools for mental health professionals* (pp. 31–55). Hoboken, NJ: Wiley.

Boyle, S. W., Hull, G. H., Mather, J. H., Smith, L. L., & Farley, O. W. (2008). *Direct practice in social work* (2nd ed.). Boston: Allyn & Bacon.

Bradshaw, J. (1972). A taxonomy of social need. In G. McLachlan (Ed.), *Problems and progress in medical care: essays on current research* (pp. 71–82). London: Oxford University Press.

Brehm, S. S., & Brehm, J. W. (1981). *Psychological reactance: A theory of freedom and control.* New York: Academic Press.

Britton, P. C., Williams, G. C., & Conner, K. R. (2008). Self-determination theory, Motivational Interviewing, and the treatment of clients with acute suicidal ideation. *Journal of Clinical Psychology, 64*(1), 52–66.

Brody, A. E. (2009). Motivational interviewing with a depressed adolescent. *Journal of Clinical Psychology, 65,* 1168–1179.

Brookfield, S. (1995). *Becoming a critically reflective teacher.* San Francisco: Jossey-Bass.

Brown, L. K., & Lourie, K. J. (2001). Motivational interviewing and the prevention of HIV among adolescents. In P. M. Monti, S. M. Colby, & T. A. O'Leary (Eds.), *Adolescents, alcohol, and abuse: Reaching teens through brief interventions* (pp. 244–274). New York: Guilford Press.

Burke, B. L., Arkowitz, H., & Menchola, M. (2003). The efficacy of motivational interviewing: A meta-analysis of controlled clinical trials. *Journal of Consulting and Clinical Psychology, 71,* 843–861.

Cain, D. J. (2007). What every therapist should know, be and do: Contributions from humanistic psychotherapies. *Journal of Contemporary Psychotherapy, 37,* 3–10.

California Evidence-Based Clearinghouse for Child Welfare (CEBC). (2006–2009). Retrieved on February 1, 2010, from *www.cachildwelfareclearinghouse.org.*

Campbell Collaboration (C2). (2010). Retrieved February 1, 2010, from *www.campbellcollaboration.org.*

Carey, K. B., Leontieva, L., Dimmock, J., Maisto, S. A., & Batki, S. L. (2007). Adapting motivational interventions for comorbid schizophrenia and alcohol use disorders. *Clinical Psychology: Science and Practice, 14,* 39–57.

Carroll, K. M., Ball, S. A., Nich, C., Martino, S., Frankforter, T. L., et al. (2006). Motivational interviewing to improve treatment engagement and outcome in individuals seeking treatment for substance abuse: A multisite effectiveness study. *Drug and Alcohol Dependence, 81,* 301–312.

Carroll, K. M., Libby, B., Sheehan, J., & Hyland, N. (2001). Motivational interviewing to enhance treatment initiation in substance abusers: An effectiveness study. *American Journal on Addictions, 10*, 335–339.

Carter, J., & Koutsenok, I. (2010). Combining motivational interviewing with cognitive behavioral therapy. Presentation at the 1st MI and Criminal Justice Summit conference, San Diego, CA.

Castro, F. G., Barrera, M., Jr., & Martinez, C. R., Jr. (2004). The cultural adaptation of prevention interventions: Resolving tensions between fidelity and fit. *Prevention Science, 5*, 41–45.

Catley, D., Harris, K. J., Mayo, M. S., Hall, S., Okuyemi, K. S., Boardman, T., et al. (2006). Adherence to principles of motivational interviewing and client within-session behavior. *Behavioural and Cognitive Psychotherapy, 34*, 43–56.

Cavaiolo, A., & Wuth, C. (2002). *Assessment and treatment of the DWI offender.* New York: Haworth Press.

Chaffin, M., Valle, L. A., Funderburk, B., Gurwitch, R., Silovsky, J., Bard, D., et al. (2009). A motivational intervention can improve retention in PCIT for low-motivation child welfare clients. *Child Maltreatment, 14*(4), 356–368.

Clark, A. J. (2010a). Empathy: An integral model in the counseling process. *Journal of Counseling and Development, 88*, 348–356.

Clark, A. J. (2010b). Empathy and sympathy: Therapeutic distinctions in counseling. *Journal of Mental Health Counseling, 32*, 95–101.

Clark, M. (2006). Entering the business of behavior change: Motivational interviewing for probation staff. *Perspectives: The Journal of the American Probation and Parole Association, 30*, 38–45.

Cloud, R. N., Besel, K., Bledsoe, L., Golder, S., McKieman, P., Patterson, D., et al. (2006). Adapting motivational interviewing strategies to increase posttreatment 12-step meeting attendance. *Alcoholism Treatment Quarterly, 24*, 31–53.

Cochrane Reviews. (2010). Retrieved February 4, 2010, from *www.cochrane.org/reviews*.

Colby, S. M., Monti, P. M., Barnett, N. P., Rohsenow, D. J., Weissman, K., Spirios, A., et al. (1998). Brief motivational in a hospital setting for adolescent smoking: A preliminary review. *Journal of Consulting and Clinical Psychology, 66*, 574–578.

Colby, S. M., Monti, P. M., Tevyaw, T. O., Barnett, N. P., Spirito, A., Rohsenow, D. J., et al. (2005). Brief motivational intervention for adolescent smokers in medical settings. *Addictive Behaviors 30*(5), 865–874.

Compton, B. R., Galaway, B., & Cournoyer, B. R. (2005). *Social work processes.* Belmont, CA: Brooks/Cole.

Corbett, G. (2009). What the research says about the MI "spirit" and the "competence worldview." *MINT Bulletin, 15*, 3–5.

Corcoran, J. (2005). *Building strengths and skills: A collaborative approach to working with clients.* New York: Oxford University Press.

Council on Social Work Education. (2001). *Educational policy and accreditation standards.* Alexandria, VA: Author.

Cowley, C. B., Farley, T., & Beamis, K. (2002). "Well, maybe I'll try the Pill for just a few months … ": Brief motivational and narrative-based interventions to encourage contraceptive use among adolescents at high risk for early child bearing. *Families, Systems, and Health, 20*(2), 183–204.

Cummings, S. M., Cooper, R. L., & Cassie, K. M. (2009). Motivational interviewing to affect behavioral change in older adults with chronic and acute illnesses. *Research on Social Work Practice, 19*(2), 195–204.

Daley, D. C., Salloum, I. M., Zuckoff, A., Kirisci, L., & Thase, M. E. (1998). Increasing treatment adherence among outpatients with depression and cocaine dependence: Results of a pilot study. *American Journal of Psychiatry, 155*, 1611–1613.

Dia, D.A., Simmons, C., Oliver, M., & Cooper, R.L. (2009). Motivational interviewing for intimate partner violence. In P. Lehmann & C. A. Simmons (Eds.), *Strengths based batterers intervention: A new paradigm in ending family violence* (PP. 87–112). New York: Springer.

DiStefano, G., & Hohman, M. (2007). The paradigm developmental model of treatment: A framework for treating multiple DUI offenders. *Alcoholism Treatment Quarterly, 25*(3), 133–147.

Dolgoff, R., Loewenberg, F. M., & Harrington, D. (2005). *Ethical decisions for social work practice* (7th ed.). Belmont, CA: Brooks/Cole.

Dubowitz, H. (1999). *Neglected children: Research, policy, and practice.* Thousand Oaks, CA: Sage.

Dubowitz, H. (2011). Neglect of children's health care. In J. E. B. Myers (Ed.), *The APSAC handbook on child maltreatment* (pp. 145–165). Thousand Oaks, CA: Sage.

Dubowitz, H., Newton, R. R., Litrownik, A. J., Lewis, T., Briggs, E. C., Thompson, R., et al. (2005). Examination of a conceptual model of child neglect. *Child Maltreatment, 10* (2), 173–189.

Dunn, E., Neighbors, C., & Larimer, M. E. (2006). Motivational enhancement therapy and self-help treatment for binge eaters. *Psychology of Addictive Behaviors, 20*(1), 44–52.

East, J., & Chambers, R. (2007). Courage to teach for social work educators. *Social Work Education, 26*, 81–826.

Edwards, J., & Richards, A. (2002) Relational teaching: a view of relational teaching in social work education. *Journal of Teaching in Social Work, 22*, 33–48.

Eichler, M. (2007). *Consensus organizing: Building communities of mutual self-interest.* Thousand Oaks, CA: Sage.

Elliott, D., Bjelajac, P., Fallot, R., Markoff, L., & Reed, B. (2005). Trauma-informed or trauma-denied: Principals and implementation of trauma-informed services for women. *Journal of Community Psychology, 33*(4), 471–477.

Enea, V., & Dafinoiu, I. (2009). Motivational/solution-focused intervention for reducing school truancy among adolescents. *Journal of Cognitive and Behavioral Psychotherapies, 9*, 185–198.

Engle, B., Macgowan, M. J., Wagner, E. R., & Amrhein, P. C. (2010). Markers of marijuana use outcomes within adolescent substance abuse group treatment. *Research on Social Work Practice, 20*, 271–282.

Engle, D. E., & Arkowitz, H. (2006). *Ambivalence in psychotherapy: Facilitating readiness to change.* New York: Guilford Press.

Fahy, A. (2007). The unbearable fatigue of compassion: Notes from a substance abuse counselor who dreams of working at Starbucks. *Clinical Social Work Journal, 35*, 199–205.

Feldstein, S. W., & Forcehimes, A. A. (2007). Motivational interviewing with underage college drinkers: A preliminary look at the role of empathy and alliance. *American Journal of Drug and Alcohol Abuse, 33*, 737–746.

Festinger, L. (1957). *A theory of cognitive dissonance.* Evanston, IL: Row, Peterson.

Fixsen, D. L., Naoom, S. F., Blase, K. A., Friedman, R. M., & Wallace, F. (2005). *Implementation research: A synthesis of the literature* (FMHI Publication No. 231). Tampa, FL: National Implementation Research Network.

Foley, K., Duran, B., Morris, P., Lucero, J., Baxter, B., Harrison, M., et al. (2005). Using motivational interviewing to promote HIV testing at an American Indian substance abuse treatment facility. *Journal of Psychoactive Drugs, 37*(3), 321–329.

Foote, J., DeLuca, A., Magura, S., Warner, A., Grand, A., Rosenblum, A., et al. (1999). *Journal of Substance Abuse Treatment, 17*, 181–192.

Forrester, D., McCambridge, J., Waissbein, C., Emlyn-Jones, R., & Rollnick, S. (2007). Child risk and parental resistance: Can motivational interviewing improve the practice of child and family social workers in working with parental alcohol misuse? *British Journal of Social Work*, 1–18.

Forrester, D., McCambridge, J., Waissbein, C., & Rollnick, S. (2008). How do child and family social workers talk to parents about child welfare concerns? *Child Abuse Review, 17* (1), 23–35.

Gagne, M., & Deci, E. L. (2005). Self-determination theory and work motivation. *Journal of Organizational Behavior, 26*, 331–362.

Gambrill, E. (2006). Evidence-based practice and policy: Choices ahead. *Research on Social Work Practice, 16*(3), 338–357.

Gaume, J., Bertholet, N., Faouzi, M., Gmel, G., & Daeppen, J. B. (2010). Counselor motivational interviewing skills and young adult change talk articulation during brief motivational interventions. *Journal of Substance Abuse Treatment, 39*, 272–281.

Gill, A. M., Hyde, L. W., Shaw, D. S., Dishion, T. J., & Wilson, M. N. (2008). The family check-up in early childhood: A case study of intervention process and change. *Journal of Clinical Child and Adolescent Psychology, 37*, 893–904.

Gillingham, P. (2008). Designing, implementing and evaluating a social work practice skills course: A case example. *Social Work Education, 27*, 474–488.

Glabbard, G., Beck, J., & Holmes, J. (2005). *Oxford textbook of psychotherapy.* New York: Oxford University Press.

Glynn, L. H., & Moyers, T. B. (2010). Chasing change talk: The clinician's role in evoking client language about change. *Journal of Substance Abuse Treatment, 39*, 65–70.

Goodman, L. A., & Epstein, D. (2008). *Listening to battered women: A survivor centered approach to advocacy, mental health, and justice.* Washington, DC: American Psychological Association.

Grauwiler, P. (2008). Voices of women: Perspectives on decision-making and the management of partner violence. *Children and Youth Services Review, 30,* 311–322.

Grenard, J. L., Ames, S. A. L., Wiers, R. W., Thush, C., Stacy, A. W., & Sussman, S. (2007). Brief intervention for substance use among at-risk adolescents: A pilot study. *Journal of Adolescent Health, 40,* 188–191.

Griffin, K. W., & Botvin, G. J. (2010). Evidence-based interventions for preventing substance use disorders in adolescents. *Child and Adolescent Psychiatric Clinics of North America, 19,* 505–526.

Hartzler, B., Baer, J. S., Dunn, C., Rosengren, D. B., & Wells, E. (2007). What is seen through the looking glass: The impact of training on practitioner self-rating of motivational interviewing skills. *Behavioural and Cognitive Psychotherapy, 35,* 431–445.

Helstrom, A., Hutchison, K., & Bryan, A. (2007). Motivational enhancement therapy of high risk adolescent smokers. *Addictive Behaviors, 32*(10), 2404–2410.

Hepworth, D. H., Rooney, R., H., Rooney, G. D., & Strom-Gottfried, K. (2010). *Direct social work practice: Theory and skills* (8th ed.). Pacific Grove, CA: Wadsworth Press.

Hettema, J., Steele, J., & Miller, W. R. (2005). Motivational interviewing. *Annual Review of Clinical Psychology, 1,* 91–111.

Hohman, M. M. (1998). Motivational Interviewing: An intervention tool for child welfare workers working with substance abusing parents. *Child Welfare, 77* (3), 275–289.

Hohman, M., Doran, N., & Koutsenok, I. (2009). Motivational Interviewing training in juvenile corrections in California: First year outcomes. *Journal of Offender Rehabilitation, 48* (7), 635–648.

Hohman, M., & Kleinpeter, C. (2009). Bringing up what they don't want to talk about: Use of Motivational Interviewing with adolescents in opportunistic settings. In R. Rooney (Ed.), *Strategies for work with involuntary clients* (2nd ed., pp.293–305). New York: Columbia University Press.

Hohman, M., Kleinpeter, C., & Loughran, H. (2005). Enhancing motivation, strengths, and skills of parents in the child welfare system. In J. Corcoran (Ed.), *Building strengths and skills* (pp. 268–292). New York: Oxford University Press.

Hohman, M., Roads, L., & Corbett, R. (2010). Initial validation of a subtle trauma screening scale embedded in a needs assessment given to women entering drug treatment. *Journal of Dual Diagnosis, 6,* 2–15.

Hohman, M., & Salsbury, L. (2009). Motivational interviewing and child welfare: What have we learned? *ASPAC Advisor, 21*(2), 2–6.

Holder, H. D., Gruenewald, P. J., Ponicki, W. R., Treno, A. J., Grube, J. W., Saltz, R. F., et al. (2000). Effect of community-based interventions on high-risk drinking and alcohol-related injuries. *Journal of the American Medical Association, 284,* 2341–2347.

Hong, S., Giannakopoulos, E., Laing, D., & Williams, N. (1994). Psychological reactance: Effects of age and gender. *Journal of Social Psychology, 134*(2), 223–228.

Ingersoll, K. S., Wagner, C. C., & Gharib, S. (2002). *Motivational groups for community substance abuse programs.* Richmond, VA: Mid-Atlantic Addiction

Technology Transfer Center, Center for Substance Abuse Treatment (Mid-ATTC/CSAT).

Interian, A., Martinez, I., Rios, L. I., Krejci, J., & Guarnaccia, P. J. (2010). Adaptation of a motivational interviewing intervention to improve antidepressant adherence among Latinos. *American Psychological Association*.

International Federation of Social Workers (IFSW). (2004). Ethics in social work, statement of principles. Retreived February 1, 2010, from *www.ifsw.org/cm_ data/Ethics_in_Social_Work_Statement_of_Principles_-_to_be_publ_205. pdf*.

Jasiura, F., Hunt, W., & Urquhart, C. (in press). Integrating motivational interviewing and empowerment groups for women. In C. C. Wagner & K. S Ingersoll, *Motivational interviewing in groups*. New York: Guilford Press.

Jenny, C., et al. (2007). Recognizing and responding to medical neglect. *Pediatrics, 120*, 1385–1389.

Kaplan, S., Engle, B., Austin, A., & Wagner, E. F. (2011). Applications in schools. In S. Naar-King & M. Suarez (Eds.), *Motivational interviewing with adolescents and young adults* (pp. 158–164). New York: Guilford Press.

Kelly, A. B., & Lapworth, K. (2006). The HYP program—Targeted motivational interviewing for adolescent violations of school tobacco policy. *Preventive Medicine, 43*, 466–471.

Kirschenbaum, H., & Jourdan, A. (2005). The current status of Carl Rogers and the person-centered approach. *Psychotherapy: Theory, Research, Practice, Training, 42*, 37–51.

Kirst-Ashman, K., & Hull, C. (2008). *Understanding generalist practice* (5th ed.). Belmont, CA: Thomson Brooks/Cole.

LaChance, H., Ewing, S. W. F., Bryan, A. D., & Hutchison, K. E. (2009). What makes group MET work?: A randomized controlled trail of college student drinkers in mandated alcohol diversion. *Psychology of Addictive Behaviors, 23*, 598–612.

Lacher, I. (2010, December 26). The Sunday conversation: Deepak Chopra. *Los Angeles Times*. Retrieved January 4, 2011, from *www.latimes.com/entertainment/news/la-ca-conversation-20101226,0,33558554.story*.

Lapham, S. C., Smith, E., C'de Baca, J., Chang, I., Skipper, B. J., Baum, G., et al. (2001). Prevalence of psychiatric disorders among persons convicted of driving while impaired. *Archives of General Psychiatry, 58*, 943–949.

LeCroy, C. W. (2002). *The call to social work: Life stories*. Thousand Oaks, CA: Sage.

Leffingwell, T. R., Neumann, C. A., Babitzke, A. C., Leedy, M. J., & Walters, S. T. (2007). Social psychology and motivational interviewing: A review of relevant principles and recommendations for research and practice. *Behavioural and Cognitive Psychotherapy, 35*, 31–45.

Levy, M. D., Ricketts, S., & Le Blanc, W. (2010). Motivational interviewing training at a state psychiatric hospital. *Psychiatric Services, 61*, 204–205.

Lincourt, P., Kuettel, T. J., & Bombardier, C. H. (2002). Motivational interviewing in a group setting with mandated clients: A pilot study. *Addictive Behaviors, 27*, 381–391.

Longabaugh, R., Zweben, A., Locastro, J. S., & Miller, W. R. (2005). Origins, issues, and options in the development of the combined behavioral intervention. *Journal of Studies on Alcohol Supplement, 15*, 179–187.

Longshore, D., & Grills, C. (2000). Motivating illegal drug use recovery: Evidence for a culturally congruent intervention. *Journal of Black Psychology, 26* (3), 288–301.

Loughran, H. (2011). *Understanding crisis therapies: A guide to crisis intervention approaches.* London: Jessica Kingsley.

Lowman, J. (1996) Characteristics of exemplary teachers, in M. D. Svinicki & R. J. Menges (Eds.), *Honoring exemplary teaching: New directions for teaching and learning,* San Francisco: Jossey-Bass.

Lundahl, B., & Burke, B. L. (2010). The effectiveness and applicability of motivational interviewing: A practice-friendly review of four meta-analyses. *Journal of Clinical Psychology: In Session, 65*, 1232–1245.

Lundahl, B., Kunz, C., Tollefson, D., Brownell, C., & Burke, B. L. (2010). Meta-analysis of motivational interviewing: Twenty-five years of research. *Research on Social Work Practice, 20*, 137–160.

Madras, B., Compton, W., Avula, D., Stein, J., Clark, H., & Stegbauer, T. (2009). Screening, brief interventions, referral to treatment (SBIRT) for illicit drug and alcohol use at multiple healthcare sites: Comparison at intake and 6 months later. *Drug and Alcohol Dependence, 99*(1), 280–295.

Madson, M. B., Bullock, E. E., Speed, A. C., & Hodges, S. A. (2009). Development of the client evaluation of motivational interviewing. *Motivational Interviewing Network of Trainers Bulletin, 15*(1), 6–8.

Madson, M. B., Loignon, A. C., & Lane, C. (2009). Training in motivational interviewing: A systematic review. *Journal of Substance Abuse Treatment, 36*, 101–109.

Manthey, T. (2009). Training motivational interviewing in a vocational rehabilitation context. *MINT Bulletin, 15*(1), 9–13.

Manthey, T., Jackson, C., & Evans-Brown, P. (2010). *Motivational interviewing and vocational rehabilitation: A literature review and implementation model for an evidence-based practice.* Manuscript under review.

Markland, D., Ryan, R. M., Tobin, V. J., & Rollnick, S. (2005). Motivational interviewing and self-determination theory. *Journal of Social and Clinical Psychology, 24*, 811–831.

Martin, G., & Copeland, J. (2008). The adolescent cannabis check-up: Randomized trial of a brief intervention for young cannabis users. *Journal of Substance Abuse Treatment, 34*(4), 407–414.

Martino, S. (2007). Contemplating the use of motivational interviewing with patients who have schizophrenia and substance use disorders. *Clinical Psychology: Science and Practice, 14*, 58–63.

Martino, S., Ball, S. A., Gallon, S.L., Hall, D., Garcia, M., Ceperich, S., et al. (2006). *Motivational interviewing assessment: Supervisory tools for enhancing proficiency.* Salem, OR: Northwest Frontier Addiction Technology Transfer Center, Oregon Health and Science University.

Martino, S., Ball, S., Nich, C., Frankforter, T. L., & Carroll, K. M. (2009). Correspondence of motivational enhancement therapy integrity ratings among therapists, supervisors, and observers. *Psychotherapy Research, 19*, 181–193.

Martino, S., Carroll, K., Kostas, D., Perkins, J., & Rounsaville, B. (2002). Dual diagnosis motivational interviewing for substance-abusing patients with psychotic disorders. *Journal of Substance Abuse Treatment, 23*, 297–308.

Martino, S., & Moyers, T. B. (2008). Motivational interviewing with dually diagnosed patients. In H. Arkowitz, H. A. Westra, W. R. Miller, & S. Rollnick (Eds.), *Motivational interviewing in the treatment of psychological problems* (pp. 277–303). New York: Guilford Press.

McCambridge, J., Slym, R., & Strang, J. (2008). Randomized controlled trial of motivational interviewing compared with drug information and advice for early intervention among young cannabis users. *Addiction, 103*(11), 1809–1818.

McDermott, M., & Garofalo, J. (2004). When advocacy for domestic violence backfires: types and sources of victim disempowerment. *Violence against Women, 10*, 1245–1266.

McLeod, A. M., Hays, D. G., & Chang, C. Y. (2010). Female intimate partner violence survivors' experiences with accessing resources. *Journal of Counseling and Development, 88*, 303–311.

McRoy, R. G. (2007). Cultural competence with African Americans. In D. Lum (Ed.), *Culturally competent practice: A framework for understanding diverse groups and justice issues*. Belmont, CA: Thomson.

Miller, E. T., Turner, A. P., & Marlatt, G. A. (2001). The harm reduction approach to the secondary prevention of alcohol problems in adolescents and young adults: Considerations across a developmental spectrum. In P. M. Monti, S. M. Colby, & T. A. O'Leary (Eds.), *Adolescents, alcohol, and substance abuse* (pp. 58–79). New York: Guilford Press.

Miller, W. R. (1983). Motivational interviewing with problem drinkers. *Behavioural Psychotherapy, 11*, 147–172.

Miller, W. R. (1996). Motivational interviewing: Research, practice, and puzzles. *Addictive Behaviors, 21*, 835–842.

Miller, W. R. (Ed.). (2004). *COMBINE monograph series: Vol. 1. Combined behavioral intervention manual: A clinical research guide for therapists treating people with alcohol abuse and dependence* (DHHS Publication No. [NIH] 04-5288). Bethesda, MD: National Institute on Alcohol Abuse and Alcoholism.

Miller, W. R., & Baca, L. M. (1983). Two-year follow-up of bibliotherapy and therapist-directed controlled drinking training for problem drinkers. *Behavior Therapy, 14*, 441–448.

Miller, W. R., Benefield, R. G., & Tonigan, J. S. (1993). Enhancing motivation for change in problem drinking: A controlled comparison of two therapist styles. *Journal of Consulting and Clinical Psychology, 61*, 455–461.

Miller, W. R., & Brown, J. M. (1994). What I want from treatment scale. Retrieved February 12, 2010, from *casa.unm.edu/inst/What%20I%20Want%20From%20Treatment.pdf*.

Miller, W. R., C' de Baca, J., Matthews, D. B., & Wilbourne, P. L. (2001). Personal values card sort. Retrieved January 4, 2011, from *casaa.unm.edu/inst/Personal%20Values%20Card%20Sort.pdf*.

Miller, W. R., Hendrickson, S. M. L., Venner, K., Bisono, A., Daugherty, M., &

Yahne, C. (2008). Cross-cultural training in motivational interviewing. *Journal of Teaching in the Addictions, 7*, 4–15.

Miller, W. R., & Mount, K. A. (2001). A small study of training in motivational interviewing: Does one workshop change clinician and client behavior? *Behavioural and Cognitive Psychotherapy, 29*, 457–471.

Miller, W. R., & Moyers, T. B. (2006). Eight stages in learning motivational interviewing. *Journal of Teaching in the Addictions, 5*, 3–17.

Miller, W. R., Moyers, T. B., Amrhein, P., & Rollnick, S. (2006). A consensus statement on defining change talk. *MINT Bulletin, 13*, 6–7.

Miller, W. R., & Rollnick, S. (1991). *Motivational interviewing: Preparing people to change addictive behavior*. New York: Guilford Press.

Miller, W. R., & Rollnick, S. (2002). *Motivational interviewing: Preparing people for change* (2nd ed.). New York: Guilford Press.

Miller, W. R., & Rollnick, S. (2009). Ten things that motivational interviewing is not. *Behavioral and Cognitive Psychotherapy, 37*, 129–140.

Miller, W., & Rose, G. (2009). Toward a theory of motivational interviewing. *American Psychologist, 64*, 527.

Miller, W., & Sovereign, R. (1989). The check-up: A model for early intervention in addictive behaviors. In T. Loeberg, W. R. Miller, P. E. Nathan, & G. A. Marlatt (Eds.), *Addictive behaviors: Prevention and early intervention* (pp. 219–231). Amsterdam: Swets & Zeitlinger.

Miller, W. R., Toscava, R. T., Miller, J. H., & Sanchez, V. (2000). A theory-based motivational approach for reducing alcohol/drug problems in college. *Health Education and Behavior, 27*, 744–759.

Miller, W. R., Villanueva, M., Tonigan, J. S., & Cuzmar, I. (2007). Are special treatments needed for special populations? *Alcoholism Treatment Quarterly, 25* (4), 63–78.

Miller, W. R., Yahne, C. E., Moyers, T. B., Martinez, J., & Pirritano, M. (2004). A randomized trial of methods to help clinicians learning motivational interviewing. *Journal of Consulting and Clinical Psychology, 72* (8), 1050–1062.

Mitcheson, L., Bhavsar, K., & McCambridge, J. (2009). Randomized trial of training and supervision in motivational interviewing with adolescent drug treatment practitioners. *Journal of Substance Abuse Treatment, 37*, 73–78.

Monti, P. M., Colby, S. M., & O'Leary, T. A. (Eds.). (2001). *Adolescents, alcohol, and substance abuse: Reaching teens through brief interventions*. New York: Guilford Press.

Motivational Interviewing and Intimate Partner Violence Workgroup. (2010). Guiding as practice: Motivational interviewing and trauma informed-work with survivors of intimate partner violence. *Partner Abuse, 1*(1), 92–104.

Moyers, T. B. (2004). History and happenstance: How motivational interviewing got its start. *Journal of Cognitive Psychotherapy: An International Quarterly, 18*, 291–298.

Moyers, T. B., Manuel, J. K., Wilson, P. G., Hendrickson, S. M. L., Talcott, W., & Durand, P. (2007). A randomized trial investigating training in motivational interviewing for behavioral health providers. *Behavioural and Cognitive Psychotherapy, 36*, 149–162.

Moyers, T. B., Martin, T., Houck, J. M., Christopher, P. J., & Tonigan, J. S. (2009). From in-session behaviors to drinking outcomes: A causal chain for motivational interviewing. *Journal of Consulting and Clinical Psychology, 77,* 1113–1124.

Moyers, T. B., Martin, J. K., Catley, D., Harris, K. J., & Ahluwalia, J. S. (2003). Assessing the integrity of motivational interviewing: Reliability of the motivational interviewing skills code. *Behavioural and Cognitive Psychotherapy, 31,* 177–184.

Moyers, T. B., Martin, J. K., Miller, W. R., & Ernst, D. (2010). Revised global scales: Motivational interviewing treatment integrity 3.1.1. Retrieved September 27, 2010, from *casaa.unm.edu/download/miti3_1.pdf on.*

Moyers, T. B., Martin, T., Christopher, P. J., Houck, J. M., Tonigan, J. S., & Amrhein, P. C. (2007). Client language as a mediator of motivational interviewing efficacy: Where is the evidence? *Alcoholism: Clinical and Experimental Research, 31,* (S3), 40S–47S.

Moyers, T. B., Martin, T., Manuel, J. K., Hendrickson, S. M. L., & Miller, W. R. (2005). Assessing competence in motivational interviewing. *Journal of Substance Abuse Treatment, 28,* 19–26.

Moyers, T. B., Miller, W. R., & Hendrickson, S. M. L. (2005). How does motivational interviewing work?: Therapist interpersonal skill predicts client involvement within motivational interviewing sessions. *Journal of Consulting and Clinical Psychology, 73,* 590–598.

Moyers, T. B., & Rollnick, S. (2002). A motivational interviewing perspective on resistance in psychotherapy. *In Session: Psychotherapy in Practice, 58,* 185–193.

Mullen, E. J., & Bacon, W. (2006). Implementation of practice guidelines and evidence-based treatments: A survey of psychiatrists, psychologists, and social workers. In A. R. Roberts & K. Yeager (Eds.), *Foundations of evidence-based social work practice* (pp. 81–92). New York: Oxford University Press.

Mullins, S. M., Suarez, M., Ondersma, S. J., & Page, M. C. (2004). The impact of motivational interviewing on substance abuse treatment retention: A randomized control trial of women involved with child welfare. *Journal of Substance Abuse Treatment, 27,* 51–58.

Musser, P. H., & Murphy, C. M. (2009). Motivational interviewing with perpetrators of intimate partner abuse. *Journal of Clinical Psychology: In Session, 65,* 1218–1231.

Musser, P. H., Semiatin, J. N., Taft, C. T., & Murphy, C. M. (2008). Motivational interviewing as a pre-group intervention for partner-violent men. *Violence and Victims, 23,* 539–557.

Myers, S. (2000). Empathic listening: Reports on the experience of being heard. *Journal of Humanistic Psychology, 40,* 148–173.

Naar-King, S., & Suarez, M. (2011). *Motivational interviewing with adolescents and young adults.* New York: Guilford Press.

Naar-King, S., Templin, T., Wright, K., Frey, M., Parsons, J. T., & Lam, P. (2006). Psychosocial factors and medication adherence in HIV positive youth. *AIDS Patient Care and STDs, 20,* 44–47.

National Association of Social Workers (NASW). (2008). Code of ethics. Retrieved January 19, 2010, from *www.socialworkers.org/pubs/code/code.asp.*

National Registry of Evidence-Based Programs and Practices (NREPP). (2010). Retrieved February 1, 2010, from *www.nrepp.samhsa.gov.*

Newbery, N., McCambridge, J., & Strang, J. (2007). "Let's talk about drugs" pilot study of a community-level drug prevention intervention based on motivational interviewing principles. *Health Education, 107*, 276–288.

Norcross, J. C. (2001). Purposes, processes and products of the task force on empirically supported therapy relationships. *Psychotherapy, 38*, 345–356.

Northern, H. (1995). *Clinical social work: Knowledge and skills* (2nd ed.). New York: Columbia University Press.

Nowicki, S., Duke, M. P., Sisney, S., Strickler, B., & Tyler, M. A. (2004). Reducing the drop-out rates of at-risk high school students: The Effective Learning Program (ELP). *Genetic, Social, and General Psychology Monographs, 130*, 225–239.

Nurius, P. S., & Macy, R. J. (2010). Person-oriented methods in partner violence research: Distinct psychosocial profiles among battered women. *Journal of Interpersonal Violence, 25*, 1064–1093.

Obama, B. (2007). *Dreams from my father: A story of race and inheritance.* New York: Crown.

Ogedegbe, G., Schoenthaler, A., Richardson, T., Lewis, L., Belue, R., Espinosa, E., et al. (2007). An RCT of the effect of motivational interviewing on medication adherence in hypertensive African Americans: Rationale and design. *Contemporary Clinical Trials, 28*(2), 169–181.

Owen, K. (2007). *The use of motivational interviewing with survivors of domestic violence.* Unpublished thesis, San Diego State University.

Payne, M. (2005). *Modern social work theory* (3rd ed.). Chicago: Lyceum Books.

Perry, C. L., Williams, C. L., Veblen-Mortenson, S., Toomey, T. L., Komro, K. A., Anstine, P. S., et al. (1996). Project Northland: Outcomes of a communitywide alcohol use prevention program during early adolescence. *American Journal of Public Health, 86*, 956–965.

Peterson, P., Baer, J., Wells, E., Ginzler, J., & Garrett, S. (2006). Short-term effects of a brief motivational intervention to reduce alcohol and drug risk among homeless adolescents. *Psychology of Addictive Behaviors, 20*, 254–264.

Phelan, M., Slade, M., Thornicroft, G., Dunn, G., Holloway, F., Wykes, T., et al. (1995). The Camberwell Assessment of Need: The validity and reliability of an instrument to assess the needs of people with severe mental illness. *British Journal of Psychiatry, 167*, 589–595.

Picciano, J. F., Roffman, R., Kalichman, S. C., & Walke, D. D. (2007). Lowering obstacles to HIV prevention services: Effects of a brief, telephone-based intervention using motivational enhancement therapy. *Annals of Behavioral Medicine, 34* (2), 177–187.

Proctor, E. K. (2006). *Implementing evidence-based practice in social work education: Principles, strategies, and partnerships.* Paper presented at the Symposium on Improving the Teaching of Evidence-Based Practice: University of Texas at Austin School of Social Work.

Reed, M. B., & Aspinwall, L. G. (1998). Self-affirmation reduces biased processing of health-risk information. *Motivation and Emotion, 22*, 99–132.

Resnicow, K., Davis, R. E., Zhang, G., Konkel, J., Strecher, V. J., Shaikah, A. R., et al. (2008). Tailoring a fruit and vegetable intervention on novel motivational constructs: Results of a randomized study. *Annuals of Behavioral Medicine, 35*, 159–169.

Resnicow, K., DiIorio, C., Soet, J. E., Borrelli, B., Hecht, J., & Ernst, D. (2002). Motivational interviewing in health promotion: It sounds like something is changing. *Health Psychology, 21*, 444–451.

Resnicow, K., Jackson, A., Wang, T., De, A. K., McCarty, F., Dudley, W. N., et al. (2001). A motivational interviewing intervention to increase fruit and vegetable intake through Black churches: Results of the eat for life trial. *American Journal of Public Health, 91* (10), 1686–1693.

Rogers, A. T. (2010). *Human behavior in the social environment* (2nd ed.). New York: Routledge.

Rogers, C. R. (1951). *Client-centered therapy*. Boston: Houghton-Mifflin.

Rogers, C. R. (1957). The necessary and sufficient conditions of psychotherapeutic personality change. *Journal of Consulting Psychology, 2,* 95–103.

Rogers, C. R. (1959). A theory of therapy, personality and interpersonal relationships as developed in the client-centered framework. In S. Koch (Ed.), *Psychology: A study of science: Formulations of the person and social context* (Vol. 3, pp. 184–256). New York: McGraw-Hill.

Rollnick, S., Miller, W. R., & Butler, C. C. (2008). *Motivational interviewing in health care: Helping patients change behavior*. New York: Guilford Press.

Rose, S. D., & Chang, H. S. (2010). Motivating clients in treatment groups. *Social Work with Groups, 33*, 260–277.

Rosengren, D. B. (2009). *Building motivational interviewing skills: A practitioner workbook*. New York: Guilford Press.

Rutledge, S. E. (2007). Single session motivational enhancement counseling to support change toward reduction of HIV transmission by HIV positive persons. *Archives of Sexual Behavior, 36*, 313–319.

Rutschman, R. (2010). Pairing motivational interviewing with adventure-challenge education. Chicago Teachers' Center. Retrieved November 28, 2010, from *www.neiu.edu/~ctc/images/pdfs/policy_brief_drop_out.*

Ryan, R. M., & Deci, E. L. (2002). Overview of self-determination theory: An organismic-dialectical perspective. In E. L. Deci & R. M. Ryan (Eds.), *Handbook of self-determination research* (pp. 3–33). Rochester, NY: University of Rochester Press.

Sakamoto, I., & Pitner, R. O. (2005). Use of critical consciousness in anti-oppressive social work practice: Disentangling power dynamics at personal and structural levels. *British Journal of Social Work, 35*, 435–452.

Saleeby, D. (2006). *The strengths perspective in social work practice* (4th ed.). New York: Longman.

Santa Ana, E. J., Wulfert, E., & Nietert, P. J. (2007). Efficacy of group motivational interviewing (GMI) for psychiatric inpatients with chemical dependence. *Journal of Consulting and Clinical Psychology, 75*, 816–822.

Scheafor, B. W., & Horejsi, C. R. (2007). *Techniques and guidelines for social work practice* (8th ed.). Boston: Pearson Press.

Schoener, E. P., Madeja, C. L., Henderson, M . J., Ondersma, S. J., & Janisse, J. J. (2006). Effects of motivational interviewing training on mental health therapist behavior. *Drug and Alcohol Dependence, 82*, 269–275.

Scott, S., & Dadds, M. R. (2009). Practitioner review: When parent training doesn't work: Theory-driven clinical strategies. *Journal of Child Psychology and Psychiatry, 50*, 1441–1450.

Shafer, M. S., Rhode, R., & Chong, J. (2004). Using distance education to promote the transfer of motivational interviewing skills among behavioral health professionals. *Journal of Substance Abuse Treatment, 26*, 141–148.

Sherman, D. K., & Cohen, G. L. (2006). The psychology of self-defense: Self-affirmation theory. In M. P. Zanna (Ed.), *Advances in experimental psychology* (Vol. 38, pp. 183–242). San Diego, CA: Academic Press.

Slade, M., Phelan, M., Thornicroft, G., & Parkman, S. (1996). The Camberwell Assessment of Need (CAN): comparison of assessments by staff and patients of the needs of the severely mentally ill. *Social Psychiatry and Psychiatric Epidemiology, 31*, 109–113.

Slade, M., Thornicroft, G., Loftus, L., Phelan, M., & Wykes, T. (1999). *CAN: The Camberwell Assessment of Need. A comprehensive needs assessment tool for people with severe mental illness.* London: Gaskell.

Smith, D. C., Hall, J. A., Jang, M., & Arndt, S. (2009). Therapist adherence to a motivational interviewing intervention improves treatment entry for substance-misusing adolescents with low problem perception. *Journal of Studies on Alcohol and Drugs, 70*, 101–105.

Smith, D. C., Motl, R. W., Elliott, J. R., Dlugonski, D., Leigh, M., & Cleeland, L. (2010). *A randomized proof of concept trial of motivational interviewing to increase exercise adherence among individuals with multiple sclerosis.* Poster session presented at the annual meeting of the MI Network of Trainers, San Diego, CA.

Spiller, V., & Guelfi, G. P. (2007). Motivational interviewing in the criminal justice system. In G. Tober & D. Raistrick (Eds.), *Motivational dialogue: Preparing addiction professionals for motivational interviewing practice* (pp. 151–162). London: Routledge.

Steele, C. M. (1988). The psychology of self-affirmation: Sustaining the integrity of the self. In L. Berkowitz (Ed.), *Advances in experimental and social psychology* (Vol. 21, pp. 261–302). San Diego, CA: Academic Press.

Stephens, R. S., Roffman, R. A., Fearer, S. A., Williams, C., Picciano, J. F., & Burke, R. S. (2004). The Marijuana Check-up: Reaching users who are ambivalent about change. *Addiction, 99*(10), 1323–1332.

Sue, S. (1998). In search of cultural competence in psychotherapy and counseling. *American Psychologist, 53*, 440–448.

Swan, M., Schwartz, S., Berg, B., Walker, D., Stephens, R., & Roffman, R. (2008). The teen marijuana check-up: An in-school protocol for eliciting voluntary self-assessment of marijuana use. *Journal of Social Work Practice in the Addictions, 8*, 284–302.

Swartz, H. A., Zuckoff, A., Grote, N. K., Spielvogle, H. N., Bledsoe, S. E., Shear, M. K.., et al. (2007). Engaging depressed patients in psychotherapy: Integrating techniques from motivational interviewing and ethnographic interviewing to improve treatment participation. *Professional Psychology: Research and Practice, 38*, 430–439.

Tollison, S. J., Lee, C. M., Neighbors, C., Neil, T. A., Olson, N. D., & Larimer,

M. E. (2008). Questions and reflections: The use of motivational interviewing microskills in a peer-led brief alcohol intervention for college students. *Behavior Therapy, 39*, 183–194.

Trauer, T., Tobias, G., & Slade, M. (2008). Development and evaluation of a patient-rated version of the Camberwell Assessment of Need Short Appraisal Schedule (CANSAS-P). *Community Mental Health Journal, 44*, 113–124.

Tsai, A. G., & Wadden, T. A. (2009). Treatment of obesity in primary care practice in the United States: A systematic review. *Journal of General Internal Medicine, 24*, 1073–1079.

Turnell, A. (2010). Signs of Safety. Retrieved September 27, 2010, from *www.signsofsafety.net/signsofsafety.*

Urquhart, C., & Jasiura, F. (2010). Introductory and advanced motivational interviewing: Supporting change and preventing FASD. Presentation to Healthy Child Manitoba, Winnipeg.

U.S. Department of Health and Human Services, Administration for Children and Families. (2005). *Child treatment.* Washington, DC: U.S. Government Printing Office.

Vader, A. M., Walters, S. T., Prabhu, G. C., Houck, J. M., & Field, C. A. (2010). The language of motivational interviewing and feedback: Counselor language, client language, and client drinking outcomes. *Psychology of Addictive Behaviors, 24*, 190–197.

Vansteenkiste, M., & Sheldon, K. M. (2006). There's nothing more practical than a good theory: Integrating motivational interviewing and self-determination theory. *British Journal of Clinical Psychology, 45*, 63–82.

Vaughan, B., Levy, S., & Knight, J. R. (2003). Adolescent substance use: Prevention and management by primary care clinicians. *Journal of Clinical Outcomes Management, 10*, 166–174.

Velasquez, M. M., Maurer, G. G., Crouch, C., & DiClemente, C. C. (2001). *Group treatment for substance abuse: A stages-of-change therapy manual.* New York: Guilford Press.

Velasquez, M. M., Stephens, N. S., & Ingersoll, K. (2006). Motivational interviewing in groups. *Journal of Groups in Addiction and Recovery, 1*, 27–50.

Velasquez, M. M., von Sternberg, K., Johnson, D. H., Green, C., Carboni, J. P., & Parsons, J. T. (2009). Reducing sexual risk behaviors and alcohol use among HIV-positive men who have sex with men: A randomized clinical trial. *Journal of Consulting and Clinical Psychology, 77* (4), 657–667.

Venner, K. L., Feldstein, S. W., & Tafoya, N. (2006). Native American motivational interviewing: Weaving Native American and western practices. Albuquerque: Authors. Retrieved March 3, 2010, from *casaa.unm.edu/nami.html.*

Venner, K. L., Feldstein, S. W., & Tafoya, N. (2007). Helping clients feel welcome: Principles of adapting treatment cross-culturally. *Alcoholism Treatment Quarterly, 25*, 11–30.

Villanueva, M., Tonigan, S. J., & Miller, W. R. (2007). Response of Native American clients to three treatment methods for alcohol dependence. *Journal of Ethnicity in Substance Abuse, 6*(2), 41–48.

Wagner, C. C., & Ingersoll, K. S. (in press). *Motivational interviewing in groups.* New York: Guilford Press.

Wagner, C. C., & Sanchez, F. P. (2002). The role of values in motivational interviewing. In W. R. Miller & S. Rollnick, *Motivational interviewing: Preparing people for change* (2nd ed., pp. 284–298). New York: Guilford Press.

Wahab, S. (2005a). Motivational interviewing holds potential for practice with survivors of domestic violence. *Arete, 29*, 11–22.

Wahab, S. (2005b). Motivational interviewing and social work practice. *Journal of Social Work, 5*, 45–60.

Wahab, S. (2006). Motivational interviewing: A client centered and directive counseling style for work with victims of domestic violence. *Arete, 29*(2), 11–22.

Wahab, S., Menon, U., & Szalacha, L. (2008). Motivational interviewing and colorectal cancer screening: A peak from the inside out. *Patient Education and Counseling, 72*, 210–217.

Walker, D., Roffman, R., Stephens, R., Wakana, K., & Berghuis, J. (2006). Motivational enhancement therapy for adolescent marijuana users: A preliminary randomized controlled trial. *Journal of Consulting and Clinical Psychology, 74*, 628–632.

Walker, R., Logan, T. K., Clark, J. J., & Leukefeld, C. (2005). Informed consent to undergo treatment for substance abuse: a recommended approach. *Journal of Substance Abuse Treatment, 29*, 241–251.

Wenzel, S. L., D'Amico, E. J., Barnes, D., & Gilbert, M. L. (2009). A pilot of a tripartite prevention program for homeless young women in the transition to adulthood. *Women's Health Issues, 19*, 193–201.

Winters, K. C., & Leitten, W. (2007). Brief intervention for drug-abusing adolescents in a school setting. *Psychology of Addictive Behaviors, 21*, 249–254.

Winters, K. C., Leitten, W., Wagner, E., & Tevyaw, T. O. (2007). Use of brief interventions for drug abusing teenagers within a middle and high school setting. *Journal of School Health, 77*, 196–206.

Woller, K. M., Buboltz, W. C., & Loveland, J. M. (2007). Psychological reaction: Examination across age, ethnicity, and gender. *American Journal of Psychology, 120*, 15–24.

Woodruff, S., Edwards, C., Conway, T., & Elliott, S. (2001). Pilot test of an internet virtual world chat room for rural teen smokers. *Journal of Adolescent Health 29* (4), 239–243.

York, B. (2008). What did Obama do as a community organizer? Retrieved March 25, 2010, from *article.nationalreview.com/370073/what-did-obama-do-as-a-community-organizer/byron-york*.

Yu, J., Clark, L. P., Chandra, L., Dias, A., & Lai, T. F. L. (2009) Reducing cultural barrier to substance abuse treatment among Asian Americans: A case study in New York City. *Journal of Substance Abuse Treatment, 37*, 398–406.

Zerler, H. (2009). Motivational interviewing in the assessment and management of suicidality. *Journal of Clinical Psychology: In Session, 65*, 1207–1217.

Zweben, A., & Zuckoff, A. (2002). Motivational interviewing and treatment adherence. In W. R. Miller & S. Rollnick, *Motivational interviewing: Preparing people for change* (pp. 299–319). New York: Guilford Press.

Index

Page numbers followed by *f* indicate figure; *n* indicate note; and *t* indicate table.